TIGERS
THE SECRET LIFE

TIGERS
THE SECRET LIFE

VALMIK THAPAR

PHOTOGRAPHS BY

FATEH SINGH RATHORE

Rodale Press

Emmaus Pennsylvania

To my parents, Raj and Romesh Thapar,
whom I miss dearly

First published in Great Britain 1989 by
Elm Tree Books

Book design by Jim Taggart

Map by Chartwell Illustrators

Published in 1989 in the United States of America by
Rodale Press, Inc.
33 E. Minor St.
Emmaus, PA 18098

If you have any questions or comments concerning this book,
please write:
Rodale Press
Book Reader Service
33 East Minor Street
Emmaus, PA 18098

ISBN 0–87857–865–X hardcover
2 4 6 8 10 9 7 5 3   hardcover

Typeset by Wyvern Typesetting Ltd
Printed in Italy

Distributed in the book trade by St. Martin's Press

Frontispiece: One of Noon's cubs sidles up to her, resting his chin on his mother's
face. She opens her mouth in annoyance. The early morning sun has broken through
over the hills and the tigers glow in the warm light.

Author's Note

This book on the tiger is the third I have written since 1982. It has probably been the most difficult and challenging and reveals some new information on the tiger for the first time.

Tigers: The Secret Life is based primarily on Fateh's and my observations, and sometimes on the information provided by drivers and forest guards, especially as we were keeping touch with three different families in three locations. Sometimes we have deduced events of the night from the evidence we had discovered in the morning. The ages of the cubs should be correct to within a month of the given figure. I have endeavoured to be as careful and accurate as possible in recounting my observations.

It was after a decade of continuous observations of the tigers in the Ranthambhore National Park that we were able to get regular insights into the family life of tigers. We were fortunate to find three tigresses and their cubs during the course of early 1986 to August 1988. This provided a basis for comparison especially in relation to the resident male tigers in their areas and their role in raising the family. The monsoons tend to make Ranthambhore inaccessible for three months. This becomes the 'missing period' in our observations but we were lucky, as Laxmi's cubs were six months older than Noon's and what we missed in this period with Laxmi's cubs we were able to observe with Noon's; this enabled us to document every month in the life of the cubs till sub-adulthood. We had struggled for many years to photograph a tigress and her young cubs, but rarely had we been successful. I think that by 1986 recording this invisible facet of their life had become an obsession for Fateh and me.

The photographs in this book have been taken using Nikon F3 and Nikon FM2 cameras with 85 f1.4, 135 f2, 180 f2.8 and 300 f4.5 Nikkor lenses. Over the years Fateh and I have developed complete faith in the performance of the Nikon system. We have primarily used Kodachrome 64 and Kodachrome 200 which are our favourite films but there have been times because of severe shortages of film that we have had to use Fujichrome 100 and 400 and at times even Ektachrome 100.

In the body of literature that exists on the tiger, the biggest gap has been a detailed natural study on their family life and facets of this have remained hidden from most naturalists for centuries. Tigers enjoy a complete sense of privacy when with a family. The over-protective nature of a tigress makes her more evasive and nocturnal when with cubs. We were lucky.

Acknowledgements

Ranthambhore National Park is one of the finest tiger habitats in the world. Living and working there is an experience that no words can describe. I am indebted to Fateh Singh Rathore, the then Field Director and my 'tiger guru', for his unmatched experience and assistance, to the Rajasthan Wildlife Department and V. D. Sharma, the Chief Wildlife Warden, for his support, to forest guards like Badhyaya, Ghaffar, Ramesh, Bahadur and Saed for their endless pursuits of tigers and to drivers like Manohar and Shafiq who were always around to provide valuable information.

My special thanks to Malvika Singh who, despite being burdened with work, managed to spend time sorting out and bringing some order to the manuscript. To Peter Lawton a debt of gratitude for his tireless efforts to push and encourage and set a pace that saw this book to completion. Tejbir Singh I must thank for not only filming some of these startling events in the book, but for some of his splendid pictures. The generosity and hospitality of Avani Patel in Ranthambhore and of Goverdhan Singh Rathore who kept me company through some of my most exciting encounters I cannot forget. I remember with warmth the young 'cubs' who in unknown ways added new dimensions in our lives – to Jaisal, Aamana, Sonali, Hannah, India, Vivaswath, Raj, Avani, Stefano and many others.

I thank N. K. Pillai for his endless hours spent in typing the manuscript, Peter Jackson, Chairman of the International Cat Group, for his comments on the manuscript and Caroline Taggart for her immediate encouragement.

Finally I must express a debt of gratitude, which is inadequate, to two special people who made this task possible, people I don't have to name.

For me this book is a realisation of a dream. I dreamt of the family life of tigers, never really expecting to document it. It has happened. Fateh and I are beholden to Laxmi, Noon and Nalghati who accepted our presence and permitted us to record facets of their secret and intimate lives.

Contents

Foreword
by H.R.H. The Duke of Edinburgh

By 1973 it had become clear that the tiger population in India was in a serious state of decline and unless some drastic action was taken there was a real risk that it might become extinct.

What was then known as the World Wildlife Fund, now WWF–World Wide Fund for Nature, and the International Union for the Conservation of Nature and Natural Resources persuaded the Government of India to join in a major rescue effort under the banner of 'Operation Tiger'. The project has been successful in saving the tiger from extinction, but in the meantime the human population of India has increased substantially and many new problems have arisen.

One of the most important features of this book is that it addresses the critical problem of human pressure on the remaining wild lands, which has now become a worldwide anxiety. Ranthambhore is a perfect example of the dilemma for people who have to graze their cattle to maintain even a basic level of life. The temptation to exploit the lush grasses of the reserve is difficult to resist when the land around has already been picked clean. This clash of interests inevitably puts a great strain on the relationship between the conservation authorities and the local people. The author puts forward some valuable proposals to ease this problem.

This book is one of the most important ever published on the subject of tigers. Observations of the family life of tigers, such as are recorded here, have never been made before. The author witnessed quite extraordinary scenes, which he vividly describes.

I found this book particularly interesting as I had the great good fortune to visit Ranthambhore nearly thirty years ago, while it was still in the possession of the late Maharajah of Jaipur. I am glad to see that the author describes the Ranthambhore National Park as 'one of the finest tiger habitats in the world'. I hope it will remain that way for many years into the future.

Noon with her five month old cub. The high grass at the edge of the lake camouflages the tigers and enables them to hide and attack the deer that come to graze.

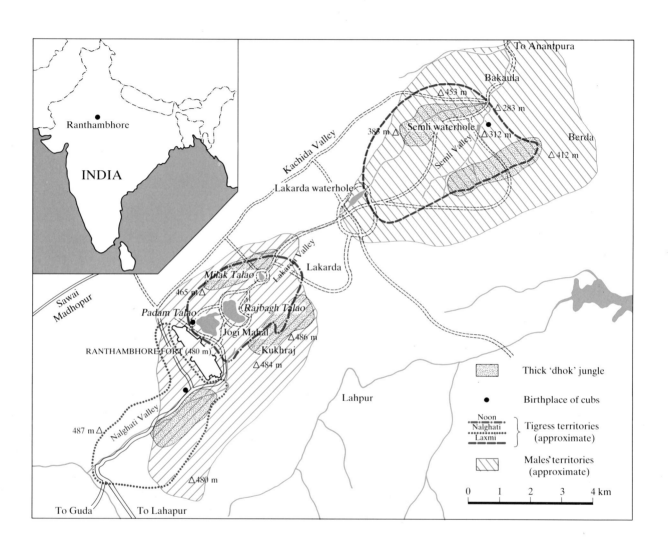

INDIA

Ranthambhore

To Anantpura

Bakaula

△ 453 m

△ 283 m

383 m △   Semli waterhole   △ 312 m   Berda

Kachida Valley   Semli Valley   △ 412 m

Lakarda waterhole

Lakarda Valley   Lakarda

Milak Talao   465 m △

Padam Talao   Rajbagh Talao

Sawai   Jogi Mahal

Madhopur   △ 486 m

RANTHAMBHORE FORT (480 m)   Kukhraj

△ 484 m

Lahpur

487 m △   Nalghati Valley

△ 480 m

To Guda   To Lahapur

Thick 'dhok' jungle

●   Birthplace of cubs

Noon
Nalghati   Tigress territories
Laxmi   (approximate)

Males' territories
(approximate)

0   1   2   3   4 km

Introduction

I think I first came under the tiger's spell 25 years ago, at the age of ten. I was in Corbett National Park, in the lower Himalaya of North India, astride an elephant. It was early morning and ten elephants were sweeping through high grass in an effort to spring some tigers into a clearing on the far side. I remember looking down and seeing a tigress snarling up at the elephant I was on, and then darting away with two large cubs at her heels. I was mesmerised, and in later years I remembered every second of this very vivid experience. It seemed etched forever on my mind.

It was thirteen years after this encounter that I saw my next tiger in the

In a rare play of light after a thunderstorm, the forest of Ranthambhore glows against a setting sun.

11

wild. Ranthambhore was then a wildlife reserve in south-western Rajasthan, sprawling over 400 square kilometres. Its dry, deciduous forest engulfed me: low rolling hills, open grasslands, steep cliffs, and the crumbling ruins of a historic past dotted around, all merged in perfect harmony, a harmony that held me spellbound. The reserve derives its name from the fortress of Ranthambhore, over a hundred metres high and seven kilometres in circumference: the forest was, in times gone by, the private hunting reserve of the Maharajahs of Jaipur. They would hunt tiger and other game for six weeks a year and for the rest of the time the area was protected. This saved it from complete destruction.

Nearly a thousand years old, the massive battlements of Ranthambhore enclose one of India's most ancient fortresses. The control of this fortress was vital to the control of central India. Countless battles have raged around these walls and the great Mughal emperor Akbar laid siege here. Lake palaces, tombs, summer gardens, temples, mosques, step wells and hunting towers, all reminders of the past, have now been overrun by grasses and shrubs, and mosses and lichens have carpeted the stone walls. Today leopards and tigers prowl the ruins.

In India in the 1960s the tiger was struggling to survive. It was only in 1970 that the ban on tiger hunting became effective. Tigers had been hunted mercilessly for the last hundred years. At the turn of the present century there were about 40,000 tigers in India. A population census conducted in India during 1973 revealed that the population had declined to about 1,800, although all figures of tiger populations are estimates, and I was later to discover that they could suffer from quite substantial margins of error. By 1973 an international campaign by the World Wildlife Fund and the International Union for Conservation of Nature and Natural Resources (IUCN) was in full swing and India launched a comprehensive conservation programme called 'Project Tiger'. Ranthambhore with fourteen tigers was the smallest of nine chosen tiger habitats.

When I first went to Ranthambhore in 1976, the forest was teeming with wildlife: deer, antelope, wild boar, crocodile, leopard, sloth bear and of course, the elusive tiger. For twenty days I roamed the forest hoping to catch a glimpse of the tiger. I saw fresh signs of it – pug marks on forest tracks, droppings, the occasional roar – but it was only on my last night that I finally encountered one striding down a forest track. I am still fascinated by this image of the tiger. I knew then that the forest of Ranthambhore and the tiger were to be a part of my life. It was the beginning of an endless pursuit to observe and discover more about what was, at that time, one of the world's most elusive, evasive and nocturnal predators.

I started spending more and more time in the park, learning about the ways of the forest. I also discovered my tiger guru. Fateh Singh Rathore, the Warden and Director of the Park, was an imposing figure, with a large bushy moustache, a stetson cap, and a sparkle in his eye. A man with many years' experience and a finely tuned instinct about the tiger and everything that lived under the forest canopy, he was a master of fieldcraft and the language of the forest. We spent endless days criss-crossing the area on foot and by jeep. Tiger sightings were few: brief glimpses mainly at night or early in the morning. At this time Ranthambhore contained sixteen villages: about 1,500 people and 3,000 domestic livestock shared the area with its wild inhabitants. One of the major aims of Project Tiger was to resettle these villages outside the forest. During those early years this was the most complicated task faced by the forest staff. Removing the human disturbance from the park would restore the equilibrium for nature. By 1978 Fateh had resettled twelve villages. The other four villages were just within the outer boundaries of the park and not so much of a disturbance. The plan to resettle them has met with delays and they still await relocation.

Tiger observations continued to be rare but we found a tigress whom we observed more regularly than most. We named her Padmini, after a queen who conquered the largest fortress in India, Chittorgarh. She had five cubs in one litter, an unusually large number to have survived the first months in the wild. Usually a tigress is seen accompanied by one, two or, at most, three cubs. One of Padmini's cubs, a female whom we called Laxmi, named after the goddess of wealth, gradually grew more confident in our presence. But lengthy observations were impossible and the tigers would melt away on our arrival. Four of Padmini's cubs survived till maturity and by late 1978 they had separated from their mother to lead their own independent lives. We had seen glimpses of family life but been totally frustrated in our attempts to document and observe any detail.

The 1980s arrived and tiger sightings increased. A slow change seemed to be taking place. The tiger was shedding its nocturnal cloak, and seemed more comfortable during the day. The primary reason for this seemed to be the resettling of the villages. The threat of man had finally been removed. Cubs had become adults, mothers and fathers, in a world where man no longer encroached or disturbed. No longer did the tiger have to evade man by seeking the shelter of the night. In 1981 we rediscovered Padmini with another litter, consisting of a male and two female cubs. Observations were still brief but the two females, whom we later named Noon (as she was unusually active in the after-noon) and Nalghati (after the valley in which she was resident) showed no fear of us humans. In 1982 we also glimpsed Laxmi with her first litter. But when she has cubs a tigress is careful and eludes observation. New glimpses into family life became more frequent, but without daily or regular encounters. Fateh and I were patient. We hoped that one day this secret life would unfold.

From 1982 to 1986 the forest quite suddenly exploded with tiger

Noon crosses the rise of a hill.
In the right hand corner is one
of the entrance gates to the
fort from where, centuries
ago, horses and elephants
must have rushed into battle.

activity. In fact Ranthambhore emerged as the only habitat in the world where the tiger was rewriting its own natural history. New and unknown facets of tiger behaviour were seen and recorded. In 1982–83 we recorded instances of communal feeding where nine tigers shared a carcass, controlled by the tigress Padmini. In fact six of these tigers were cubs of Padmini's litters. The adults and sub-adults of three generations had come together. It was the first sign that tigers might sustain kin links throughout their lives. This was a rare encounter. There is no record in the last fifty years of similar gatherings of tigers over food. At the end of the last century and early this century some sportsmen did describe large gatherings of tigers, but such encounters occurred during hunts using artificial baiting, not in a natural situation. I think our observation is the only existing natural record of tigers sustaining their kin links. It changed the usually held belief that tigresses keep no contact with their adult cubs. I think that tigers, either as siblings or as cubs and parents, recognise one another if and when they meet. Such meetings do not seem to be regular, however, and may occur once or twice a year.

For the first time we recorded details of the tiger's range and territory, marking, patterns of vocalisation, feeding habits, predation and hunting techiques, dominance and submission behaviour and finally even courtship and mating.

By 1985 our discoveries about tiger behaviour, and about their associations with other denizens of the forest kept us busy with note-book and camera. For the first time tourism flourished in the area. Endless jeeps roamed the forest in their quest for tigers. When a tiger was sighted, in no time at all, ten jeeps would appear. Shades of East Africa. But under such human pressure the tiger tends to retreat and our efforts to study new facets of behaviour suffered. We now invariably attempted to 'hide' ourselves in the jungle if we were with tigers.

I have never seen tigers mating, but after twenty years in Ranthambhore Fateh was lucky enough to document Noon and the male tiger Kublai courting and mating. It was the summer of 1985 and we hoped that Noon would conceive, since we had never seen her with cubs. She was nearly four years old.

But this did not happen. We had, over the years, been fortunate in gaining glimpses of family life, but there remained a gaping void in our knowledge of the tiger. We had no detailed record of the first eight to ten months in a tiger's life. Despite an endless pursuit of tigresses with cubs, the forest cover would finally make them invisible. By 1986 we were in close touch with three tigresses, Laxmi, Noon, and Nalghati, but none of them had cubs. Our sightings of them were regular and on occasions we could spend most of a day observing them.

Ranthambhore had now been accorded national park status and had become one of the most important tiger habitats in the world, a place

Two sambar hinds graze in the waters of Rajbagh at dawn on a cloudy morning.

where tigers could be seen regularly and in the day time. But with this success new problems arose. Over the last decade sharp increases in domestic livestock, combined with the growing human population, have exerted a tremendous pressure on the park, for its 'fodder' and wood. Successive droughts had made life difficult for the 40,000 people around the park. A series of encounters between the forest staff and the rural communities strained vital relationships. The people had become alienated from the forest. More graziers and wood cutters entered the park, illegally, doing a lot of damage. I wondered whether the forest and its inhabitants could survive this tremendous pressure even for another decade. It was probably Project Tiger's biggest error, that little had been done for the people in all these years. If wildlife is to survive, man and nature must find a harmonious balance.

Early in 1986 I realised that it was nearly ten years since I had visited Ranthambhore for the first time. I had learnt a great deal from the finely tuned senses of Fateh and his uncanny instinct which had led us into innumerable tiger encounters. He could interpret the tell-tale signs of the forest: understanding the nuances of scare calls, the indentations on the forest floor, scratch marks on trees, the odour of a tiger's marking; following crows, tree pies and vultures to the source of their frenzy. We had become expert in the use of our eyes, ears and nose, in order to assess, absorb and pursue our objective. There were successes and failures but Fateh's instincts were remarkable. He could suddenly change his mind and take off in a different direction within the forest, and would usually end up finding tigers. His detailed knowledge of the terrain, from patches of grass to rocks and boulders, water holes, caves, streams and ravines enabled him to take his jeep into areas which no one else would even think of investigating.

Over these years Fateh and I spent long hours arguing about tigers and their behaviour, sleepless nights worrying about their fate and the future of Ranthambhore. As director of the park Fateh had managed to create conditions that made Ranthambhore one of the finest natural habitats in which to view and study the tiger. A well protected forest, a successful village resettlement scheme, an efficient forest staff, important research programmes, and the large network of two hundred and fifty kilometres of forest roads had contributed to the development of the area. But with its success came serious problems: a deteriorating relationship between the rural communities and the park, and a sharp increase in tourism. I think the latter really escalated when Prime Minister Rajiv Gandhi spent the New Year of 1986 in the park with family and friends. Ranthambhore was flashed all over the country as an important location and hordes of people arrived after Mr Gandhi's departure to see the 'spot'. Uncontrolled tourism can severely disturb the harmony of a forest and this was a source of concern to us in the early part of that

year. In addition to the tourists, the park is regularly visited by pilgrims on their way to the fort: as many as a thousand pilgrims cross the park every Wednesday, and the total number varies from 5,000 to 8,000 each month.

I had, over the last ten years, seen the tigers of Ranthambhore evolve, increase and become completely fearless of human observers. This change had been captured in two books and four films on the tigers of Ranthambhore. I had written endless articles on the area's ecological system. But now the time had come to tackle the critical problem of the people and livestock versus the park. We held a series of meetings with the Department of Wildlife to try to find ways of relieving this incessant pressure on the park. We also sent a note to the Prime Minister outlining the park's problems. I knew that the time had come to act before it was too late. I could no longer sit back and simply observe the wildlife. Something had to be done for the rural communities around the park. It

An early winter's morning at the edge of the lake. The mist slowly recedes, revealing the ramparts of the fort. A flock of greylag geese fly into the mist. This is the magic of this wilderness area where history and nature have merged to create a unique, evocative and fragile oasis.

One of the largest banyan trees in India, located near Jogi Mahal. This tree is recorded in the writings of a Moghul emperor of 500 years ago. Shady and vast, its canopy provides a home for a thriving bird population, and occasionally tigers can be seen passing under it.

was the first time that Fateh and I thought of starting a non-governmental organisation for the sole purpose of increasing the harmony between man and nature.

In March 1986 I was in Delhi, musing over the problems of the park, when late one evening a Swiss photographer arrived at the door with an urgent message from Fateh. Laxmi had been seen with three two-months-old cubs during the day and it appeared that they were frequently to be seen in the valley of Semli. The Swiss photographer had even taken the first picture of Laxmi and one of her cubs. Fateh suggested I come immediately. I couldn't believe it. Could this be what we had been waiting for all these years? I left the next day for Ranthambhore, my heart pounding with excitement.

The Tigress and Her Cubs

The valley of Semli is in the heart of the forest. It is rarely visited by tourists and remains relatively undisturbed. At one corner of the valley is an underground spring that creates a small stream and flows into a ravine, thick with grass, trees and water. Since this is a vital source of water, the area attracts chital and sambar deer, the occasional chinkara or Indian gazelle and troops of langur monkeys that feed on the many fruit trees in the vicinity. It is also a good area for sloth bears that are drawn to the fruit. Strangely enough it was in the valley of Semli that two of our most exciting encounters took place. The first was in 1979 when we spent most of a night with a leopard and her two cubs.

One of Laxmi's cubs, three months old, stalks forward towards a partridge. Even at this age the cub's instincts, which will finally turn it into one of the world's most powerful predators, are apparent: it even stalks towards our jeep under the watchful eye of its mother.

The leopard had killed a spotted deer or chital but before the family could eat, a hyena appeared and fought off the leopard, annexing the carcass. The leopard tried to retrieve it, but after a fight was forced up a tree to watch the hyena below, gorging himself on the deer. Because of the inaccessibility of the thick forest, such encounters are rare and have seldom been recorded. On another occasion we witnessed our first kill when a tiger sprang out of the grass and fell upon an unsuspecting chital. These experiences live within us even today.

This area has steep sharp cliffs, and narrow gorges, creating belts of excellent leopard country. Natural caves abound and though leopard sightings in Ranthambhore are very rare, especially since the increase in tiger sightings, it is here that the leopards live.

The valley of Semli leads to the ravine of Bakaula on one side and on the other lie the undulating hills of Lakarda. Laxmi was the resident tigress of Lakarda and Semli and her home range stretched across ten square kilometres. The resident male of the area was the Bakaula male, his range encompassing 22 square kilometres. Several tigresses live within the range of one male tiger and besides Laxmi, the Bakaula female and another tigress had their smaller home ranges in this area. Tigers prefer to lead solitary lives and within the home range of a male tiger there is little interaction between the females. They stick meticulously to their areas. This is made possible most effectively through scent marking. A tiger raises its tail and shoots out a fluid which is a mixture of urine and a secretion from the anal glands. Another tiger reacts to the smell by hanging its tongue out and wrinkling up its nose. This gesture is referred to as 'flehmen'. The smell can last for a few days to a few weeks. It is an excellent indication to tigers of how recently another has passed by and whether the area is occupied or not. This therefore discourages interaction or, in the case of two dominant males, may encourage possible conflict. A tigress in oestrus will attract a male tiger by the scent which pinpoints her position: she will wander throughout her home range calling and marking with great frequency. Specific trees and bushes that demarcate a tiger's range are spray marked regularly. Even claw marks on the bark of a tree act as territorial signals. The tiger is normally a silent animal, but vocalisations are also a form of communication between males or between a male and a female, and are vital between a tigress and her cubs.

Many thoughts of tigers and their behaviour filled my mind as I roamed the Semli Valley, hoping to catch a glimpse of the cubs. I was convinced that Laxmi must have mated with the resident Bakaula male. Fateh's record of Noon and Kublai mating is fascinating. In 88 minutes he watched the tigers copulate eight times. The insertion is only for fifteen to twenty seconds, the process noisy and aggressive. Violent aggression can end the sexual act. The tigress snarls viciously, twists around and slaps the male away from her. Earlier she will have encouraged him by provocative movements, nuzzling, rubbing flanks; the time between copulation is spent in much love play, licking and nuzzling. Tigresses that do not conceive can come into oestrus again thirty to ninety days later. The gestation period is from 95 to 115 days and the bulge of the tigress's belly is only clearly visible in the last few days of her pregnancy. At this point she disappears from sight, and from our previous experience, sometimes remains unseen with her brood for ten to twelve months.

Early one morning, I was driving through the Semli Valley, wondering if Laxmi would show herself again. Dawn is a special time, the play of light, wafting mist, the cool fragrant air, all clothing the forest with an unmatched perfection. Suddenly I noticed the forest track was covered with fresh pug-marks. I examined them. A large tigress with her tapering pad, followed by a mass of tiny pug marks, her brood, had walked ahead of us some minutes ago. They must be around. Could they be just ahead of me? It would be unusual for Laxmi to walk such young cubs down an open track. Usually this does not happen till the cubs are four to five months old. I inched the jeep forward, my eyes scanning both sides of the track for a glimpse of the family.

A few hundred metres ahead I stop the jeep. It is time to wait for sounds of alarm. In the distance two sambar hinds move gingerly away, tails half raised. A chital looks sharply towards the forest. It is motionless. My eyes are unable to pick out anything. The shrill alarm of a peacock breaks the silence. Another peacock picks up the call. After a few seconds the alarm call of the chital pierces my ears. Frenzied and frequent calling now surrounds me. Quietly I watch the forest. It seems as if the tigers are walking towards the vehicle track. Suddenly shades of tan and black emerge from the dull yellow of the forest. Laxmi appears with three tiny cubs. One of the cubs jumps across the road. It looks about two and a half to three months old. I can hardly believe my eyes. It is my first glimpse ever of cubs this size. Laxmi settles down on the track for a few minutes. Her cubs look at me furtively from the cover of a bush. She soon rises and paces leisurely into the forest, followed by three scampering cubs. They move towards a network of ravines and disappear from sight. For me it is a dream come true. I rush back to base, heart pounding with excitement. In near hysteria I tell Fateh what I have seen. We sit down to plan strategies for the following weeks.

Observing tigers involves tremendous patience and resources of sensitivity and concern in order not to disturb the animal unduly. These

THIS PAGE:
Laxmi has just killed a chital or spotted deer stag near the Semli water hole. Startled at our sudden appearance, she grabs it by the neck and, half straddling it with her forepaws, drags the kill off. The deer is fully grown but still light enough to be carried away in this fashion. Tigers prefer to eat in thick cover, away from scavenging birds and animals.

OPPOSITE:
The cubs are about three months old. Laxmi reclines and licks them vigorously. At this age, licking is important for the cubs' bodily functions, bowel movements and circulation. After a few minutes, Laxmi leads the cubs to the kill. It is the first time we have seen cubs of this age feeding from a carcass. Their continuous diet of milk is being supplemented by meat.

needs are heightened a hundred fold when observing a tigress with cubs. Firstly, the cubs are vulnerable when small and the tigress can be aggressive. One has therefore to keep a certain distance so as not to intrude into the tiger's privacy. This causes problems in photographing them. But in this unique situation photography was secondary. The difficulties had to be overcome slowly: our first strategy was to build a confidence between us and the tigers.

I wondered what the cubs must have experienced over the last two months. There are no records of any observation of cub birth in the wild. Most of the information comes from captivity. The tigress chooses a thick bush or cave, secure and inaccessible to intruders, to deliver her cubs. A litter can be born in an hour but can sometimes take as long as 24 hours. The process is exhausting for the tigress and she gets some nourishment from the placenta and embryonic sac which she eats.

A tigress can deliver up to seven cubs and the sex ratio is one to one at birth. Mortality is high and usually two to three cubs survive the first few days. Some cubs are born dead, others die soon after birth. They are born blind and completely helpless. The eyes open three to fourteen days later, but clear vision does not come for a few weeks. In the first days the tigress must assist her cubs to find her teats, to provide them with their vital nourishment. Odour must play a critical role in this link with the mother, especially before the eyes open. The cubs remain within the security of the den and the tigress is devoted to their needs and ready to defend them against any danger from predators or scavengers. Laxmi must have had to hunt to feed herself close to the den but the spot was chosen carefully and the presence of deer and antelope in the vicinity was assured because of the water hole.

These first days in the life of the cubs are nerve-racking for the tigress. She treats any intrusion into the area around her cubs with great suspicion. If she feels disturbed or insecure for some reason she is likely to change her den by carrying each cub, one at a time, in her mouth, holding them gently by the head with her canines and molars.

Sometimes a tigress can shift her den four or five times in the first month. She spends a lot of time keeping her cubs warm and licking them vigorously, to stimulate them to defecate or urinate and for better circulation. All this activity happens without the male who fathered the litter. She is alone in providing this care and protection. The male tiger leaves soon after mating and has always been believed to be a danger to the cubs, often killing them if he has the chance. The tigress is therefore forced to protect her cubs against the male tiger.

The cubs spend their first eight weeks in and around the den. Soon they become frisky, exploring the area of the den and playing with each other. They quickly establish a teat order and gradually, a hierarchy

OPPOSITE:
Nalghati's six month old male cub atop a low branch of a tree. Young cubs beginning to explore their mother's range seem to delight in climbing trees. Their light bodies enable them to clamber up rapidly, almost leopard-like in their movements.

OVERLEAF:
Laxmi's four month old cub peers from behind a bush. In these first few months, the cubs have an insatiable curiosity about the new sights and sounds that they absorb with the passage of each day.

amongst themselves. The tigress instils a sense of order and discipline by the occasional snarl, cough or growl. After two months their regular diet of milk is supplemented by meat and the tigress carries and drags parts of what she has killed to the den.

The next morning I find Laxmi sitting in a grass patch ten to fifteen metres from the forest track. Her three cubs surround her. One nuzzles her face, another rests against her back, the third watches us curiously. Very tentatively it moves a little towards us before rushing back to the security of Laxmi. The cubs now turn their attention on each other, leaping into the air and knocking into each other. They then dash towards Laxmi. She licks one of them thoroughly, then lies on her side to suckle them. All three soon find the right teat and feed, stimulating the flow of milk with their tiny paws. For fifteen minutes I watch this remarkable spectacle. I have never seen such a display of love and warmth, such evidence of a strong bond between a tigress and her cubs.

In the next days we encountered the family regularly in Semli, getting closer and closer to them each time. Laxmi was unconcerned about our presence in the jeep. Fateh had joined me and our cameras clicked away. The cubs got bolder, and one of them, the most confident, even approached to within a metre of our jeep. A secret life that we had only speculated about was suddenly unfolding before our very eyes. It was at this point that we discovered the sexes of the cubs. Two females and one male.

One afternoon I found Laxmi just after she had killed a chital stag. She dragged it quickly in leaps and bounds up the rise of a hill and into thicker forest. Of the cubs there was no sign. In ten minutes she came out of the forest and walked a hundred metres towards a network of ravines. I decided to follow, taking the jeep off the track, cross-country. In minutes she had approached a small ravine and began calling, a low 'aooo', several times, and disappeared behind a bend. I took the jeep up a hill to look down. It was a gorge thirty metres long, ten metres wide, and surrounded on two sides by a cliff and rock overhang some twenty metres high. There were two caves in the cliff face and the three cubs came rushing out of one of them. Dense cover carpeted the floor of the gorge and a large pool of water reflected the light of the evening sun. A perfect hideout. Amidst a lot of 'pooking' sounds and nuzzling, the cubs followed Laxmi out of the ravine, miaouwing plaintively, as if they knew they were being led to a feast. Laxmi sat for a few minutes in a clearing to lick her cubs and soon they all strode off to where the carcass had been left. I followed through thick bush and rock, until I

could go no further. Through my binoculars I noticed that she had opened the rump of the spotted deer and the cubs had already been at it. Visibility was very poor, but it was clear that the cubs were used to meat even before the age of three months. Adult tigers begin eating from the choicest portion of the carcass, the rump, moving slowly towards the neck. Some tigers remove the stomach and intestines before eating and others don't. Cubs tend to attack whatever portion of the carcass they get to first. This was a time when communication between them increased through a series of low sounds, a cough, a moan, a squeak. An incredible variety exists in the language of the tiger!

Over the next few weeks both Fateh and I spent many days with the family in their delightful hideout, observing and documenting facets of their lives, events we had never seen before. It was April and the onset of summer. The cubs spent much of the time soaking themselves in the cool water, waiting for Laxmi. A bit of playing, some climbing and exploring, and a lot of sleeping was their daily routine.

Laxmi would spend most of the day patiently searching for prey. For many hours she would wait perfectly camouflaged near a water hole in the hope of a quick spring on an unsuspecting deer. Several times we saw her bring portions of her kill for the cubs to eat. For the cubs this

Laxmi suckles her four month old cubs. The cubs demand their mother's milk constantly and Laxmi obliges with tremendous patience. The cubs' tiny paws push outwards around their mother's belly to stimulate the flow of milk. In such a situation, the male cub tends to take the most comfortable position.

was a moment of joy: they bounded towards her, greeting her with squeaky sounds, and much licking before devouring the carcass. The cubs were becoming more adventurous, exploring the small ravine which was their hide-out, nibbling at twigs and branches, chewing whatever came their way, prodding at stones and boulders, investigating any small movement, be it insect, bird or butterfly. New sounds like the sudden booming alarm call of the sambar which had previously frightened them would now be accepted. They would raise their heads at such alarms, and the raucous barking of a troop of langurs would keep them alert and motionless. Even the shrill call of the stork-billed kingfisher needed getting used to: it was a whole new world of sight and sound.

With the remnants of kills in their hideouts the cubs would watch circling king vultures and endless crows as they attempted to land, but the gorge was too narrow for their safety. The cubs would chase the crows off their kills. The occasional mongoose that slipped in would also retreat from the ravine. For the first time these young tigers were interacting with other life in the forest.

One day I found the jeep tracks covered with pugmarks, not only those of Laxmi and her cubs but also those of a large male. On closer

Laxmi cuddles one of her four
month old cubs early one
April morning. Cuddling is a
vital assertion of close
physical bonds, and provides
an umbrella of security for the
cubs, who compete constantly
for their mother's attention.

examination I saw that it was the pug of the resident Bakaula male. The measurement of the diameter of the pad, and the fact that there was a twist to one of his toes, confirmed his identity. Pugmarks can be distinctive but when cubs of the same age walk on a track it is exceedingly difficult to distinguish them. Discerning details from pugmark is an art which requires instinct, experience and knowledge of the home range of a tiger.

I was worried and looked desperately for the family, but couldn't find them. What was the male tiger doing with them? Had he attacked them? My anxiety continued for two days till I found them all intact in their hide-out.

Some days later, on returning to base after several hours with Laxmi, I found a very excited Fateh who yelled, 'You won't believe it but I've found Nalghati with two cubs only a month older than Laxmi's.' I

Laxmi suckles and reclines with her five month old cubs at the edge of the den in which they were born. The setting is perfect: the entrance to the hide-out secure and sheltered by a curling, overhanging cliff. It is remarkable how carefully these dens are selected.

couldn't believe it. Another family! We could do a comparison of their lives.

Nalghati lived in the valley of Nalghati, a narrow stretch between two hill ranges that snaked across the edge of the fortress and carried on for some six kilometres. Nalghati valley is nearly fourteen kilometres from the valley of Semli. Here the deer and antelope are more dispersed. The area of Nalghati is the home range of the resident male Kublai. The Nalghati tigress focuses her activity in this valley and the adjoining area of the lakes is the home range of the tigress Noon. Kublai is the resident of both areas. I tried initially to divide my time between both families but it became too hectic, and in the end I left Fateh to concentrate on the Nalghati family while I remained with Laxmi.

The first time that I saw the Nalghati family was at the end of April. Mother and cubs were resting late in the evening near a water hole. The

Laxmi leads all her cubs through the forest. They are five months old and these walks within their home range familiarise the cubs with the area and all the nuances of the forest language. The cubs love these walks, rushing around with leaps and bounds, exploring new places and observing birds, animals, insects and even reptiles. They assess the terrain and accumulate a wealth of new experience.

Laxmi leads her six month old cubs through a dry stream bed. During the rains this would be a raging river. Such nallahs or dry stream beds crisscross the forest and are often used by tigers to patrol their ranges.

cubs were a little rounder than Laxmi's, about a month older. At six that evening the cubs got up and nuzzled their mother in an attempt to wake her. One of them moved to find a teat. The other watched us and moved to a tree, quickly clambering up a low overhanging branch on which he settled comfortably. Young tiger cubs enjoy climbing and playing on the branches of trees, though as they grow older and heavier they become unable to clamber up them. In the area of Semli several branches bear the signs of tiger activity, but this was the first time I had seen a cub up a tree.

The Nalghati tigress soon rose and moved to the tree on which her cub was resting. It was dusk. She lifted her tail to mark the tree and her cub patted her head with his paws. This was the male cub. The other was a female and less confident in our presence. The cub clambered down and they soon moved into thicker forest.

Fateh had examined the area of Nalghati carefully. It was, after all, the place where we had first had glimpses of Padmini and her family in 1977. The Nalghati tigress seemed to have used a large, thick green bush with a sort of cave-like entrance as her den. Nearby was a small pool of water and all around high grass. Quite secure but nothing like Laxmi's impregnable hideout.

At this time both families were quite mobile. Laxmi had started walking her cubs around three square kilometres of the Semli valley, and, watching them on these early walks, it was fascinating to see the cubs scampering about with abandon as if experiencing a totally new and free world. The Nalghati tigress was moving her cubs through a stretch of two and a half square kilometres. It started from one corner of the fortress and ran up to a deep gorge, most of the area being on either side of a vehicle track. As the cubs grew, so would the area with which they had to familiarise themselves.

One evening I found Fateh in an agitated state. He had encountered Kublai, the resident male of Nalghati, in the vicinity of the family hideout. We had both now seen signs of the presence of the resident male around the families' areas. What could this interaction be about? All past records of sportsman/naturalists and recent studies by zoologists indicated that the tigress reared her young by herself and that the male tiger was a threat to her offspring. There are in fact numerous records of male tigers killing and devouring cubs. I found only two sportsmen who differed in this view some hundred years ago; they went so far as to state that the male tiger is *not* addicted to infanticide and has in fact been observed in the company of cubs of all ages. Widely differing views without evidence, and no photographs of a male tiger with cubs in natural situations.

Fateh and I decided to concentrate our energies on this development. Could we discover more about the reason for the presence of the

The home of Laxmi's cubs. The den has water in the centre, thick grass and bush around, a cliff face on the left and the curve of a hill on the right to make it an excellent shelter. The cubs, now six months old, revisit this den, where they were born, regularly and are left for long periods to fend for themselves while Laxmi is out searching frantically for prey. It is a time when the more dominant male cub takes charge of his siblings, who follow obediently.

resident males around the families? What was the role they were playing? We had two months before the onslaught of the rains in early July. The Semli cubs were nearly four months old, the Nalghati cubs nearly five months. We had only two months left in which to record the glimpses of their early life. After the rains the cubs would be ten to eleven months old and much larger. We were not even sure whether they would all survive the monsoon.

As temperatures cross 40°C in April or May, water holes start drying up and the deer and antelope congregate in large numbers around the limited water spots, moving little in the day or night. The tiger does much the same. His mobility is reduced and dependent on the availability of water, not only for drinking but also for predation. It is a 'pinch period' as the coats of the animals get patchy and rugged. The forest and everything under its canopy seems to shrivel, sweat and melt with the onslaught of the heat. Once in a severe drought a small herd of chital, in search of water for their parched mouths, jumped into a well too deep for them, and died. Such are the pressures of the summer. The blistering heat of the next two months would take its toll on us and the cameras and film. Our objective, to increase periods of observation, would not be easy.

The Father

On 29th April Fateh found the Nalghati tigress and Kublai sitting some twenty metres from each other under the shade of the flame of the forest tree. It was the first time that they had been observed together, but of the cubs there was no sign. Their absence was a trifle worrying. The male and female spent much of their time sleeping with little evidence of conflict. Sleeping or resting is typical tiger activity on a hot day. Energy is carefully conserved.

Fateh returned the next morning to find a pair of king vultures perched high up on a tree and scores of white backed vultures at different points nearby. A pair of Egyptian vultures circled low over a

Kublai, the resident male tiger of the lake area and the Nalghati valley. He is probably the father of both Noon's and Nalghati's litters. His range encompasses nearly 30 sq. km. Here he cools off on a hot summer's day in the waters of Rajbagh.

dense grove of bushes and shrubs. Above one of these thick bushes several crows flew about in a frenzy. These were all certain indications of the presence of a carcass. Fateh decided to negotiate the difficult terrain in his jeep and soon found Kublai resting under the shade of a tree. Kublai is a medium sized male weighing some 200–225 kg. He is probably three metres in length from tip of the nose to tip of the tail. Records of the length of tigers have been known to exceed 3.5 metres and nearly 275 kg in weight. The tigress is at least 30 cm shorter and 45 kgs lighter but these are estimates: our tigers have not been measured or weighed!

After much scanning with binoculars, Fateh glimpsed the Nalghati tigress deep inside a bush, guarding the carcass of a sambar hind. It was difficult to see, but it looked as if she had eaten a small portion of the rump. Again, there was no sign of the cubs. I joined Fateh and we spent the day under the branches of a tree, watching what turned out to be one of the most exciting encounters with tigers we had ever seen.

Early in the afternoon, the tigress spent half an hour feeding on the carcass. The heat was intense, nearly 45°C. A hundred metres away there was a small water hole surrounded by large boulders. We decided to position ourselves around it. The tigers had to come to the water at some point.

At four in the afternoon Kublai lazily ambles towards the pool and slides into the water, hind legs first, soaking himself completely, leaving just his head visible. Tigers don't like water splashing in their eyes and most of them enter water backwards.

About twenty minutes later Nalghati follows and they both laze around in the water. Minutes later both my heart and Fateh's must have missed a beat. The male cub walks quite nonchalantly towards the pool, not a flicker of surprise or fear on his face, circles the two adults and enters the water near where Kublai is stretched out. Soon, following her brother, the female cub walks to the pool, entering the water to sit on her mother's paw. Nalghati licks her face. Fateh and I cannot believe our eyes – the tranquillity of the scene is extraordinary. One big happy family: Nalghati, Kublai and two five-month-old cubs all in close proximity, soaking themselves in this rather small pool of water. They lap the water at regular intervals. In half an hour the male cub rises, quickly nuzzles Kublai and leaves the pool. The female cub follows him and they play, leaping at each other, slowly drifting towards a tree, clambering up the branches to play a game of hide and seek amidst the foliage. The two adult tigers watch. Soon

This is probably one of the rarest pictures in this book. Kublai, the resident male, the Nalghati tigress and her two cubs all share a tiny pool of water, cooling off on a hot May evening. For centuries male tigers have been regarded as a threat to young cubs, but in all three families we observed, we saw the male tiger sharing his food, partaking of the tigress's and cubs' food, nuzzling the cubs and generally keeping a protective eye on them. After Nalghati left the pool, Kublai spent nearly an hour playing with the cubs. This is the first photographic record of tiger, tigress and cubs together in natural conditions.

Nalghati leaves the water and disappears into the forest. The cubs continue to play with each other under the protective eye of Kublai. At dusk, Kublai heaves himself out of the water and moves towards the cubs. The cubs rush up to him. He licks one of them.

When we leave, Kublai is sitting a metre or so from the two cubs. We have witnessed what must be one of the most closely kept secrets of a tiger's life. It is the first photographic record of a resident male associating with a tigress and her cubs in his range.

The next morning Fateh decided to go towards Semli, acting purely on instinct. I went to Nalghati but was unable to find the tigers. They must have been around since the crows and vultures were still perched on the trees. When tigers are away from their kill, vultures and crows leave their perches in the trees, dropping to the ground to consume the remnants. If they are near the carcass, tigers have been known to kill the vultures as they land, with a smack of their powerful paws. So the birds waited patiently on the trees. The dense forest cover hid the tigers. I returned to base early and Fateh rolled up an hour later, beaming. I knew immediately that something exciting had happened.

It is 1st May, 1986. Just at the edge of Semli, in the gorge of Bakaula, Fateh finds the Bakaula male and Laxmi. They are sitting on the vehicle track facing each other. On both sides of the track are thick groves of jamun, cool, lush and green. There are pools of water of various sizes nearby. Laxmi rises briefly and nuzzles the Bakaula male before moving a little way ahead to lie down on her side. A stork-billed kingfisher calls near the water. A pair of Boneli's eagles circle above a cliff.

This tranquil scene is disturbed by the distant sound of a rolling pebble. Both tigers become alert. Laxmi moves stealthily towards the sound. The Bakaula male sits up expectantly. A sambar deer shrieks in alarm. Laxmi has disturbed it. Tail raised vertically, the sambar carefully walks down an incline. Laxmi is too far away to attack. The sambar's path is taking it unknowingly towards the Bakaula male, who crouches, muscles tense. The sambar approaches the vehicle track. The male tiger takes off like a bullet. Six bounds and it leaps on to the back of the sambar, bringing it crashing down. Quickly it transfers its grip to the throat. At the same instant a group of noisy tourists arrive, stunned at seeing a male tiger choking a sambar to death bang in the middle of the vehicle track. But

the male is disturbed and walks off behind a bush. The sam-
bar is not quite dead. It twitches with small spasms of life.
Laxmi arrives.

Comfortable in the presence of jeeps, she grips the throat of
the sambar for a couple of minutes, ensures that there is no
life left in the deer and starts the tedious process of dragging
the 180 kg carcass away, a few metres at a time, into thick
cover. The Bakaula male watches her carefully. The carcass is
now some fifteen metres inside the jamun grove at the edge of
a small clearing. The tiger moves towards it. So does Fateh.
An amusing scene confronts him. The male tiger, with his
forepaws on the sambar's rump, has a firm grip on one of the
hind legs. Laxmi has a firm grip on the throat. The carcass is
stretched between the two tigers. A mock tug of war ensues as
each tries to pull the carcass a little towards them. Both tigers
emit low-pitched growls, interspersed with herculean tugs at
the carcass. Then, with a sudden burst of energy and strength,
Laxmi yanks the carcass some four metres away with the
Bakaula male astride its rump: a remarkable feat, as sambar
and tiger together must weigh about 450 kg. But it exhausts
her and she lets go of the throat. The male quickly pulls the
carcass out of sight.

Laxmi strides off. Fateh follows. She enters a dry stream bed
that leads to her den. She starts to call and is greeted by bird-
like squeaks from her cubs. The complex and elaborate
language of the tiger resonates through the atmosphere. In
minutes Laxmi returns with the cubs running around her in
circles. One of them runs between her legs and tries to leap
over her back. The other two are frisky and jump up the
trunks of trees before slowly moving to where the carcass lies.
The cubs have already learnt the art of sniffing and they
follow the drag marks of the carcass. They seem quite relaxed,
as if this wasn't the first occasion that they were going to share
a feast with the Bakaula male. The male cub suddenly sniffs
the spray mark of a tiger on a bush and wrinkles up his nose in
the gesture of flehmen. Soon they all disappear out of sight to
where the Bakaula male and the carcass lie. Within the last
two days we have twice seen a remarkable facet of the family
life of tigers: the resident male in the role of father.

After a quick breakfast Fateh and I rushed back to spend the day at
Bakaula. At two in the afternoon the Bakaula male emerged and soaked
himself in a pool of water. An hour and a half later he moved off and
Laxmi emerged with her cubs to cool off at the water's edge. All of them

Laxmi reclines with her seven month old cub near a pool of water. The cub quenches his thirst. By now, the cubs are strolling around their mother's range much more, using a series of different shelters to rest in by day. But they still prefer the familiarity of their original den, and are to be found in it two or three days a week.

looked well fed, their bellies bulging. From our past encounters we knew that there was a strict regimen in the feeding process. Most of the time the mother ensures that each cub eats separately on a carcass. This avoids the conflict that can arise over food. When one cub has had enough he normally moves off to socialise with his mother or to drink. Then the next cub comes to feed.

At four o'clock Laxmi moved away from the water to rest in a small clearing. Her cubs did not give her a moment's respite, jumping on her to find her teats. They succeeded, but within minutes Laxmi shrugged them off, rose and settled down again. The cubs continued to pester her and Laxmi snarled and rose again. This sequence was repeated several times. The cubs were into their fifth month and suckling them was now an irritation: their sharp teeth bothered their mother. For two days Laxmi, the Bakaula male and the cubs remained around the jamun

groves, cooling themselves in the water, the cubs playing around between feeds. They all slept a lot. The cubs delighted in jumping on Laxmi's tail and she flicked it around in anticipation as if she were performing a rope trick.

May and June are the months when the heat is most intense and many water holes dry up. Tigers remain close to water, moving from one water hole to another. So do all the deer and antelope. Till early June Kublai and the Bakaula male were found in frequent contact with the families in their range. Every few days their pugmarks were found together and there was evidence to suggest that both resident males were interacting with the families, particularly over food. The tigresses and cubs would join their respective resident males on a kill, or the male would invite himself to their kills. In between, the resident males would go off to patrol their ranges. There was no question, then, of the male tiger practising infanticide. We did not know what happened in the first two months of the cubs' life, but we now had evidence that in the course of the next few months the male took an active part in providing food for the cubs and their mother, and therefore had a vital role to play in raising the family. The tigress does most of the hunting, as she spends all her time with the cubs. The resident males patrol their home ranges, but when they are with the tigress and cubs, they can hunt or assist in a hunt. Of course they still need to eat themselves, but they are conscious of the demands of the cubs.

But this contradicts reports from all over India of male tigers killing and devouring their cubs. Why did this happen? Was Ranthambhore different in some way? We had posed ourselves a series of questions for which we would one day have to find some answers.

I was convinced that as far as both these families were concerned, the resident male had fathered the litter and we had seen him in the role of father to the family.

At the end of May I was back in Delhi for a few weeks when I got a cable from Fateh; it read, 'Come immediately. Noon has given birth to two cubs.' I was ecstatic. Noon was my favourite tigress and the resident of my favourite part of Ranthambhore, the lake area. This is a system of three lakes with the imposing fortress of Ranthambhore stretched around it. What had happened in the park? Three tigresses, all with cubs, when for years we had not even come close to a family! Noon's area immediately adjoined that of the Nalghati family and this meant it would be especially interesting in terms of territorial behaviour and overlaps. Kublai was also the resident male of the lake area. In Kublai's home range there were now two tigresses with cubs.

I returned to Ranthambhore on 5th June. Fateh met me at the station and explained what had happened. Three days earlier, after an uneventful morning drive, Fateh had been in the middle of breakfast when Badhyaya, the forest tracker, rushed up and said, 'Sir, there are some little cat like babies in a thick bush, five hundred metres away, the road workers have stumbled upon them.' Fateh jumped up, splashing coffee all over himself. In twenty years of tiger pursuit he had never seen newly born cubs. But they might be leopards. Camera in hand, he rushed off on foot with Badhyaya. He could not take the jeep into the bush. This put him in a dangerous situation. If you catch her unawares, a tigress with cubs will charge, especially human beings on foot. Jeeps at least they are used to. This was Noon's area and she could be quite aggressive. In five years of watching, we had never seen her with cubs, even though Fateh had recorded her mating twice.

Fateh's tension mounted as they walked into a dense ravine at the edge of the metal road that winds itself from Jogi Mahal to Sawai Madhopur. The fortress of Ranthambhore loomed overhead. A group of road workers stood in a nervous cluster pointing downwards. Fateh asked them to leave the spot and go home. Fateh and Badhyaya entered the ravine, slowly, step by step. Fateh is not easily frightened by things around him, but he did confess to me that this was the most nerve-racking moment of his life, not knowing when a tigress or leopardess might come charging out at him. But, since the cubs had been seen by the road workers, Fateh assumed that the mother was away hunting.

Paradise flycatchers flew around this evergreen area. The ravine has a perpetual supply of water and connects through an old dam to Padam Talao, the first in the series of lakes. A small stream flows through a rocky bed. The setting is very picturesque.

A couple of golden orioles flitted around a mango tree. Fateh could hear his heart pounding. They had carefully advanced thirty metres towards a thick green bush surrounded by bamboo. Badhyaya pointed excitedly but it was dark around the bush and their eyes could only adjust gradually. The tigress was still not around, but she might return at any time. Creeping forward, Fateh peered into the bush. A slight movement caught his eye. A tiny, striped head peered out and snarled: a tiger cub, as confident and aggressive as his mother. Two black-and-tan striped balls were cuddled up together, about fifteen days old, their eyes just open. Fateh quickly took some pictures of the cubs through the foliage and bamboo. A record was essential. In the distance a peacock called in alarm. The tigress might return any time and Fateh and Badhyaya retreated. Fateh still had to confirm the tigress's identity. Reaching the metal road, he quickly issued instructions to close the area to human intruders, and took a vantage point above the ravine.

A few hours later he saw Noon moving in the ravine. The identity was confirmed. Though the ravine was a perfect den for the tiny cubs, it was too close to the metal road which is the main highway to town. To close it to traffic for more than a few hours was impossible. During the next two days an endless steam of pilgrims started winding their way to the Ganesha temple, on top of the fort, to be blessed by the Gods. Roaring viciously, Noon mock charged three times. Some of the pilgrims fled. A worrying situation. The location of the den was dangerous not only for the cubs but also for people passing by.

That night Fateh was fast asleep on his roof under the open sky. In the heat of the summer this is the only way to remain cool. At 4.45 in the morning the peace and still of the night was suddenly shattered by the alarm call of a sambar and the shrill barking of a troop of langur monkeys. Fateh, jolted from sleep, tumbled out of bed and looked down. A predator was on the move. The first rays of morning light crept across the horizon. On the vehicle track below Noon was striding

Noon's cubs, fifteen to twenty days old, in the thick grove where they were born. The den is very close to the main artery that connects the forest with the nearest town, so Noon was forced a few days later to move her cubs to a new shelter. The cubs were found accidentally by road workers; Fateh, who took the picture, said he had rarely been so nervous, not knowing when Noon might return from hunting.

The Bakaula male, resident of Laxmi's territory. Notice the scars on his nose, probably acquired as a result of a conflict with another tiger. The Bakaula male must weigh over 200 kg and has to defend his home territory continuously from takeovers by other male tigers. He has now ruled his range, encompassing an area of 22 sq. km., for five years – a remarkable achievement.

along, carrying one of her tiny cubs in her mouth. Another first in Fateh's life, but alas there was no light for a photograph. Noon crossed some ruins and clambered up over an old wall, disappearing into one of the most inaccessible areas below the ramparts of the fort, a hundred metres from Fateh's room. She soon returned, crossed the track and fifteen minutes later came striding back with the second cub in her mouth. Fateh heaved a sigh of relief. The cubs were now in one of the safest places within Noon's range.

Now we had three tiger families to document: an enormous task. From then until early July, we saw Noon several times but we never glimpsed her cubs.

The Semli cubs were in their seventh month, the Nalghati cubs in their eighth. They had been weaned completely off their mothers' milk, and were growing rapidly on their continuous and regular diet of meat. Both mothers were forced to hunt every day or every other day, depending on the size of animal killed. An adult sambar can last for three or

four days, a chital one or two days, a wild boar a few hours, and so on.

Laxmi with her brood of three was forever on the prowl. The cubs' appetites had grown and they attacked ferociously and devoured whatever was presented to them. Their interactions and play had become rougher as they charged each other, tumbling and twisting in an effort to slap one another. This would finally help them in learning to hunt and defend themselves. The Nalghati tigress's male cub was the dominant one and always ate first, while his submissive sister waited her turn. He was also the more confident in our presence. In Laxmi's litter the male was the dominant one, eating first at a kill, and the female was the most curious of the lot, as far as we were concerned, approaching to within a metre or so of the jeep without any sign of fear. All the cubs still enjoyed being suckled by their mother, though I was not sure how much nourishment that provided. It seemed to be more a method of reinforcing the close bonds within the family. Both resident males were still in the vicinity.

The cubs were now learning the art of hunting. Laxmi's cubs spent much of their time stalking peafowl in the area. Bunched low, they would inch their way towards these birds, before breaking into a charge. The peafowl fled but the cubs were learning. They even chased the small red spur fowl and sometimes stalked the grey partridge. I have seen them chasing mice, hare and even squirrels. The cubs were alert to what was going on around their den. The mouth of the den led on to an open ground where chital and sambar grazed. Cloaked by the cover of leaves they alertly watched the deer or a troop of monkeys jumping from branch to branch. From this den they could peer all around and spot the occasional chinkara on an incline; birds, lizards and frogs, insects, butterflies and a variety of smaller and larger mammals were all observed and investigated from the secure cover of their hideout.

At dusk on 5th July we left Kublai in the company of the Nalghati family. The next morning dark clouds loomed. The rains were coming. Soon the vehicle tracks would be obliterated and our work would have to stop. Moving off, we suddenly encountered Kublai and Noon sitting together a short distance from where her cubs must have been. Kublai had walked about six kilometres through the night and was now consorting with the second family in his range. Again I was convinced he had fathered this litter as well. He was moving from one family to another, patrolling his range. I spent some time theorising about the male tiger, his role as father and why infanticide occurs, when it does.

My conclusion, which Fateh laughs at, as it is not based on evidence, is this. A resident male can father several litters in his range. He performs the role of father to all of them, sharing his food and sometimes feasting on theirs. A problem only arises when the resident male is usurped from his range by a new male in a territorial encounter. These encounters can be violent; tigers can limp off from them with serious injuries or are sometimes killed. When a resident male is usurped, a new tiger will be eager to mate and procreate quickly with the females in his area. This is when the cubs suffer. Similar observations have been made with troops of monkeys when male bands seize control of a troop and the new male kills the infants so as to get the harem back into oestrus. Sometimes this also occurs within lion prides. It must happen with tigers too. Of course we need many more hours of observation and concrete evidence to prove it.

Young males leave the mother when they are between twenty and 24 months old. They tend to move to the fringes of an area where they will hunt, eat and develop their size, strength and abilities. It takes a year, and sometimes two, of evasive, elusive behaviour before they mature to match the powers of the resident males.

In Ranthambhore young and sub-adult males exist within the home range of the resident male, in the park and on the fringes. Scent marks keep them away from any direct confrontation. If they happen to encounter each other, conflict is usually resolved. I have once seen an accidental encounter between two males late at night, one slightly larger than the other. They rushed at each other with the most blood chilling roars. Nose to nose they snarled ferociously, but in seconds the younger male dropped to the ground and rolled over on his back in a gesture of submission. The conflict was over and the resident male walked silently away. I think a serious problem only arises when two equally strong males compete with each other, in an assertion of a territorial right, and neither is ready to submit. In some of these encounters a tiger can be killed and even eaten by the victor. I have never found a male tiger killed by another male, but I know that a tigress once killed an adult male to protect her cubs. The male might have been an aggressive transient. His carcass had been opened and a chunk of his rump eaten. There have been several cases of adult male tigers killing and eating small male cubs in other parts of India.

It would all have to wait till the rains were over. Torrential down-pours struck the park. It rained all day without stopping. We rushed into town before the roads got completely flooded. The monsoon had arrived. The parched earth would now fill with water. The regeneration of life would start. The large herds of deer would break up, and move in twos and fours to the upper plateaus in search of fresh grass. The tiger would follow, leaving valleys which would soon brim with water. The coats of the deer would change yet again.

We would have to wait three months to resume our work. I wondered what the fate of the three families would be. Fortunately, what we might miss in the lives of the Semli and Nalghati litters, we would be able to document with Noon's cubs. We would have the opportunity to record every month in the life of a cub as it moved towards adulthood.

A Tiger's Kingdom

Ranthambhore is a tiger's kingdom. Even within its four hundred square kilometres there is great natural diversity in its topography and terrain. The two hill systems within the park create a series of valleys, most of which are occupied by resident males. Valleys like Kachida, Bakaula, Semli, Berda, Nalghati and Lahpur are also connected to each other through a network of ravines and gorges that provide day shelters for the tiger. Each of these valleys has its own nuances, which must be understood if one is to absorb the varying behaviour of the predators and prey that live in them. The lake of Gilai Sagar is a large marshy tract of water at one edge of the forest, a sharp contrast to

Greylag geese fly off into an early winter morning's mist. These migratory birds fly into Ranthambhore from colder climes like Siberia for the winter between November and March. They cackle away all day long and sometimes can be found in their hundreds.

53

Noon crosses the edge of
Padam Talao early one
winter's morning. The
Ranthambhore fort looms
behind her.

the general topography of the park. Looming above it is another deserted fortress, Khandar. This stretch of flat open land is ideal for the neelgai – the great Indian antelope – found here in large numbers. It also attracts a few thousand bar-headed geese every year; with its low-lying hills it has evolved in its own special way.

The system of three lakes that stretch around the fortress of Ranthambhore is in sharp contrast to Gilai Sagar. Not only does it appear distinctive to the naked eye, the behaviour of animals, be they predator or prey, is very different from that found in the rest of the park. The animals have had to adapt to a life built around large tracts of water. Within the waters of the lake live several species of aquatic plants, fish, soft shell turtles and over a hundred marsh crocodiles. Countless species of birds live and winter around these waters: greylag geese, black storks, saras cranes, painted storks, ibises, stilts, dabchicks, pelicans, teals, grey and purple herons, egrets, cormorants, darters, osprey, fishing eagles, serpent eagles, to mention a few. This busy and thriving ecological system exists within an area of about five square kilometres. High grass surrounds most of the lakes and large herds of sambar and chital are found concentrated there – they are more dispersed in the rest of the park. Because the area is open and less dense, small groups of neelgai and chinkara, the Indian gazelle, frequent the edges. Sounders of wild boar are a common sight. For the leopard the area provides little cover and I have never come across this predator around the lakes. The Indian sloth bear ambles about, especially when the 'ber' fruit is in season. Over the last eight years the resident tigers have adapted their hunting techniques to this area, making it a predators' paradise today.

The sambar deer have probably adapted the best to life around the lakes. Normally regarded as a shy and elusive resident of the thicker forest, here they are found in their hundreds, congregating around the lakes but more often entering the water, wading and swimming, eating the succulent plants that grow within. Their life is water-based and even the colour and condition of their coats is in sharp contrast to those that live elsewhere in the forest. Sambar are not found in such large herds anywhere else. From November through to March is their courtship season, and the stags fight for supremacy of the harems. Surprisingly, much of this activity takes place in and around the lakes. Their antlers fall off during April, May and June, and when the monsoon breaks they are in velvet, a living tissue that feeds the antlers till they are fully developed. They spend most of the wet season on the plateaus of the park. Their numbers become more concentrated around the water points as the heat intensifies and as water sources begin to dry up. Living on the aquatic plants in the lake is not without its share of danger. Adult crocodiles attempt continually to kill the deer, but are only successful when a young fawn strays into deep water. Adult sambar usually manage to escape by a great deal of kicking when there is any hint that the crocodiles may attack. But over the last few years four or five large crocodiles have played havoc with the deer, and many more sambars have fallen victim to them. This successful predation has not deterred the deer from their addiction to the water and its plants. Young fawns that grow up in the area follow their mothers into the water and somehow develop as 'water deer'.

Until the end of 1983 the sambars' only concern was with the few crocodiles that might lunge at them. In the water they were safe from tigers. This also changed with the appearance of a new resident male – Genghis – at the end of 1983. Sambar form the largest prey base for the tiger around the lakes and Genghis adapted his hunting technique masterfully by studying the sambar's addiction to the water. From the cover of high grass around the lake he would shoot out into the water, his speed and accuracy remarkable, causing total panic amongst the deer in the water. The sambar were unable to rush away easily, as they might do on dry land, and invariably young deer would fall victim to Genghis. His success rate was one in five, higher than tigers that kill on dry land. He remained around the lakes for a year, a ferocious predator. He would even take kills from the crocodiles when they were successful. But even during this period of ruthless predation, the sambar never left the waters of the lake. Genghis disappeared late in 1984 and we have never see him again. But he left behind a hunting technique that the resident tigress, Noon, had picked up, probably from watching him in action. She now became the 'water killer'. The sambar remained undeterred. I wondered what might happen when her cubs were grown. They would naturally pick up this innovative technique.

Unlike the sambar, chital never enter the water. They graze in herds at the edges. The chital court and mate in Ranthambhore throughout the year. This activity reaches a peak during March and May. Occasionally they are chased to the edges of the lake by a tiger which has been sheltering in the high grass. But being exceedingly fast on open ground, they avoid predation more successfully than the sambar. This is true only of the lake areas. In the Nalghati and Semli valleys, an equal number of chital and sambar are preyed upon, because the sambar are much more dispersed.

Other prey on the lakes are wild boar, neelgai, the occasional langur monkey and peafowl. Large populations of peafowl live around the lakes and are attacked frequently, especially if young cubs are around. Cubs learn their early hunting techniques by chasing peafowl. Nocturnal animals like the porcupine and ratel also fall victim to the tigers.

Observation of wildlife around the lakes is a naturalist's dream. The area is picturesque, scattered with ruins and a lake palace, and the ever-imposing fortress of Ranthambhore. The terrain is open, affording excellent visibility. The first lake, Padam Talao, or 'the lake of the lotus', is adjoined a hundred metres away by the second lake, Rajbagh, 'the garden of kings'. Jogi Mahal, the forest rest house, sits on the edge of Padam Talao with its terrace serving an excellent observation post. My diary record of 15th March 1982 states:

It is 8.30 a.m. and I have just returned from a morning drive. I sit out on the balcony of Jogi Mahal to have a cup of coffee. I watch a crocodile as it glides through the water. A pied kingfisher hovers above before dropping into the water like a stone, coming up again, seconds later, with a fish. The lotus is about to bloom, and most of the lake is covered with a spread of green leaves. The morning drive has been uneventful and I

A mother langur with her newborn infant. Langurs are the only primate living in Ranthambhore. They spend much of their time in trees, safe from a tiger's attack, and cackle-bark in alarm at the sight of a tiger or a leopard. Following their eyes is a great help in pinpointing the exact location of a tiger.

OPPOSITE:
A male leopard feeding on a sambar kill. A sambar is three times the size of a leopard, so the leopard must have been forced off his feet to grapple with his prey. He killed it in Laxmi's home range and eats furtively, wary of the tiger's presence. At noon he deserted the carcass and it was consumed by vultures. This was the first time in fifteen years we had observed a leopard eating an adult sambar.

wonder what the evening holds. My gaze drifts to a herd of fourteen chital grazing on the lush green grass at the edge of the lake. The coffee arrives and I take my first sip watching this serene lake and its surroundings when quite unexpectedly a cacophony of chital alarm calls diverts my attention to a tiger that has charged the herd from the tall grass, startling them into confusion and successfully catching one. The suddenness of the attack has caught me by surprise. The next moment the tiger grips the neck of the chital and carries it off into the high grass around the lake. It looks like a doe. The whole event has lasted two minutes and the lake appears to be back to its former calm and serenity.

On innumerable occasions in 1984, from the terrace of Jogi Mahal, I saw Genghis and Noon charging through the water and killing sambar. Rajbagh, the second lake, is the sambar's favourite. You can spend hours observing deer, birds, crocodiles and tigers when they are around. This lake is half a kilometre away from Malik Talao, the third and smallest lake, and the only one to dry up in early summer. Small pools of water lie between them. The area behind Rajbagh is cool and shady, like a nursery for the sambar and chital. Mothers with their young take refuge there. Vehicle tracks swing all around the lakes and the area has the disadvantage of being the most frequented by tourists. Endless jeeps whizz about and if a tiger is present it can attract up to ten vehicles. But I knew this area when few tourists came and today if there are no jeeps it is still one of the finest places to be. I have seen a tiger kill about fifty times, and on forty occasions it was in the lake area.

I once watched six crocodiles attacking a young sambar in the waters of one of the lakes, twisting and turning their bodies in an effort to yank off the limbs of the deer and amidst much splashing, tearing the carcass apart. Crocodiles are important scavengers around the lake. In May 1985 a large sambar stag collapsed and died in a sun-baked clearing at the edge of Rajbagh. The dead stag provided a focal point for four days of feeding activity in which we were able to study at close quarters the natural hierarchies and interactions of the scavengers of Ranthambhore. Early on the first morning we found the area around the carcass criss-crossed by crocodile tracks. The reptiles, whose teeth are not very sharp, had only managed to tear a chunk of flesh from the sambar's

A jackal carries off a chital fawn. When the jackal kills in Ranthambhore, he is furtive and wary of a tiger's presence. I once saw Noon attracted by scores of vultures and hundreds of crows to a place where two jackals were feeding on a chital fawn. The young tiger darted in, the jackals fled and the tiger ate. Recently Noon killed and ate a passing jackal. This was our first observation of such an incident.

Portrait of Noon.

A large sambar stag with
antlers entwined with weeds
from the lake. It is the rutting
season and sambar stags crash
their antlers into branches and
grass as they prepare to court
their harem.

neck before retreating into a nearby pool. Crocodiles find it difficult to eat on land. It was a lucky break for the vultures; white-backed, Egyptian, king, griffon and long-billed vultures all congregated to feed, tearing at the carcass through the opening made by the crocodiles and all the time flapping, kicking and fighting amongst themselves. The next morning a pair of jackals arrived on the scene, approaching cautiously and then charging the vultures, trying to find a few mouthfuls. Late in the afternoon four wild boars arrived. They approached aggressively, forcing the jackals to retreat. The boars annexed the carcass and gorged themselves. They established themselves firmly as the dominant scavengers. Vultures and jackals kept away and even the crows and tree pies found it difficult to snatch a few scraps. The wild boar is a tough animal. Even tigers keep their distance from large adult boars, especially if the tiger is at all inexperienced as a hunter. On the third morning evidence on the dusty soil indicated the arrival of a tigress. She had picked up the few remnants of bone and flesh and dragged them thirty metres away to some bushes where she had chewed and licked the bones clean. The area around the lakes had become the arena for some of my most revealing encounters with tigers.

Noon has been a resident tigress of these lakes since early 1983. She must be now between seven and eight years old and weigh close to 180 kgs. Noon has certain distinctive features. After many hours of observation you learn to recognise her facial markings over the eyes and cheek. She also has a broken right lower canine, easily visible when she yawns. Her character is different from the other tigresses we have observed. She hunts around the lakes at any time of day and probably bases her technique on the movement of the deer at the lake's edge. Unlike Laxmi, she is aggressive around a carcass, sometimes mock-charging the jeep, forcing us to keep a greater distance. She tends to favour long bursts of speed in pursuit of prey, again adapting her technique to the open land around the lake. Laxmi, on the other hand, prefers to hide in thick cover, stalk her prey slowly and attack over much shorter distances.

The Semli valley is about ten kilometres from the lakes. Its own special characteristics made it possible for us to document the early life of the cubs, as a network of ravines, lush and green, were all accessible by jeep. We could not have driven so close to the cubs in the lake area. Laxmi, the resident tigress of this valley, is nearly twelve years old and this was the second litter of hers that we had seen. She is slighter heavier and a few centimetres longer than Noon. She is also much calmer and less aggressive. Her territory has little open ground and she has adapted her hunting techniques accordingly. Unlike Noon she is much less active between midday and five o'clock.

Tigers vary enormously in their individual natures, and their

A magnificent sambar stag lit by the early morning sun at the edge of Padam Talao. An egret stands motionless on his back.

Twenty-seven Indian marsh crocodiles bask on the shore of Padam Talao. The fort looms on the horizon. There are about 150 crocodiles in the lakes and their staple diet is fish. As crocodiles grow they will start attacking young sambar fawns to supplement their diet. If an animal dies naturally on the shore of the lake it is immediately scavenged by the crocodiles. Sometimes they walk along vehicle tracks, crossing from one lake to another.

behaviour is governed by their immediate environment. The Nalghati tigress is about the same age as Noon but more heavily built. Her hunting area is the Nalghati valley, a stretch of land seven kilometres long, surrounded by steep cliffs and hills with thick lush gorges. Her periods of intense activity are the early mornings and late evenings.

At one end of her area in a deep gorge lives the only human habitant of the park, Kawaldar Baba. He spends most of his time in meditation in a small cave on a cliff face. He has in a way merged with nature. On innumerable occasions he and Nalghati have encountered each other at close quarters, and there has been no threat or sign of fear on either side.

The two resident males in our study differ considerably in size. The Bakaula male is bigger and heavier than Kublai, who is sleeker and more athletic looking. We are unsure of their ages but think that they are somewhere between seven and nine years old. Kublai is more diurnal than the Bakaula male, who tends to disappear into cover for most of the day. Both have thick ruffs of hair around their cheeks.

There are an equal number of sambar and chital in Ranthambhore.

The total figure is about 9,000. There are about 2,000 neelgai and 700 chinkara. About 1,500 wild boar roam the forests. Thousands of langur monkeys and hundreds of thousands of peafowl complete the prey base in the forest for about forty tigers and probably an equal number of leopards. Few tigers, but many more leopards prey on stray domestic livestock on the fringes of the forest. Over the years most of the leopards have been pushed to the fringes by increased tiger activity within the park. Young tiger cubs might be vulnerable to a leopard's attack, but usually leopards keep their distance. The strong scent of the tiger families must act as a deterrent. The same is true for the hyena. In Ranthambhore hyenas are found singly or in pairs but never as a pack. The total population of hyenas in the park must be about 25, and they are exceedingly difficult to see. Again, their more regular activity is around the fringes of the park, scavenging the carcasses of livestock that may have died naturally.

Traditional hunting tribes had always killed jackals and could sell their skins for a hundred rupees. Because of this the jackal population was devastated, and although a total ban on hunting jackals was imposed five years ago, it is still rarely seen. In fact we see more tigers than jackals. Once between Padam Talao and Rajbagh I encountered two jackals. They had just killed a tiny chital fawn and were in the process of tearing it apart. In minutes scores of vultures circled the area, some settling on the trees nearby. Dozens of crows watched the jackals, cawing noisily. Attracted by the sounds, Noon emerged from a bank of grass two hundred metres away. She watched the vultures and crows for a while, then strode forward to investigate. As she approached, the jackals abandoned the fawn and trotted in circles around her. Quickly she picked up the carcass and walked off to a cover of grass to eat, leaving the jackals in a frenzy of frustration.

There are about a hundred to 150 sloth bears in and around the park. The tigers and sloth bears keep their distance from each other. Unlike leopards, which are submissive with tigers, and sometimes even fall victim to them, the bear remains unperturbed and I have witnessed bears walking past tigers without any great concern. The tiger remains alert, watching them move away, but does not adopt an aggressive posture. Only once did I see Genghis, who was a particularly aggressive tiger, charge an unsuspecting sloth bear; both bear and tiger slapped each other with their forelegs and finally the bear retreated. But both seemed to respect each other's presence.

There are about 150 marsh crocodiles in Ranthambhore. Their main diet is fish, supplemented sometimes by deer. Around the park are two river systems, the Chambal and the Banas. Both have healthy populations of crocodile and gavial, and the surrounding area is protected as a national park in order to keep nesting colonies safe.

It is difficult to get accurate figures of the larger mammals and reptiles that live in and around the fringes of the park. At the height of the summer, usually in the first week of June, an annual census is conducted, primarily for the tiger but also encompassing other animals. The forest is divided into about a hundred compartments and each compartment is manned by two forest personnel. For several days all observations around the water holes of that particular compartment are recorded on a map of the area that has to be filled in. So a tiger's movements, its pugmarks, are all filled into the map, and each day's count of other animals is also recorded. It is like filling in a big jigsaw puzzle for approximately seven days. The information finally reaches the forest headquarters and an 'animal concentration' map of the park is put together for each of the seven days. The accuracy of such a method depends on the reliability of the forest personnel. It can therefore only be successful when every forest tracker and guard is highly motivated, very knowledgeable and experienced in the census area that he is assigned. He must be fully trained in the recognition and analysis of the pugmarks of all the forest animals and must be familiar with the day to day activities and movements of the tigers within his area of forest. But this is too much to expect. Recruitment into the forest service is not based on a man's interest in the tiger, or in wildlife. Many forest guards join the service because they have to earn a livelihood. Census operations tend therefore to be treated casually and suffer from large margins of error. The figures I have quoted are mere approximations of the total picture.

Late in August 1986 I visited Ranthambhore for a few days. The transformation was extraordinary. From a dull yellow at the height of the summer the forest had become a lush green. The grass was high, providing dense cover. The weather was humid, the insect life buzzing. An endless croaking of frogs and the gurgling sound of water pervaded the atmosphere. It was a great time for the reptiles. Cobras, kraits and vipers were at their most active, taking their toll of the frogs. The Indian monitor lizard streaked around the nests of birds and preyed on snakes. Many migratory birds flew in to feast on the endless dragonflies that filled the skies. Crocodile eggs were getting ready to hatch. All vehicle tracks were like streams and any depression in the ground had turned into a water hole. The network of ravines and what had been dry stream beds gushed with water. The deer and antelope were invisible, most of them on the higher reaches of the park. There were few signs of tigers. The forest guards revealed that they had had occasional glimpses of Noon around Jogi Mahal, which gave us hope that her cubs had survived the wet season. The rains had not been as good as they should have been, the water levels not as high as normal. We would not know how serious the drought was until later in the year. For now, Fateh and I could only speculate about October when we would rediscover all three families. I was convinced that Noon and her two cubs would provide us with the most rewarding encounters around the lakes, with their superb visibility and thriving prey. In fact, documenting the lives of three tigers around the lakeside, in these startling surroundings, would be a total delight. I knew that since my favourite area is the lakes, I would concentrate on Noon and her cubs from October on. Fateh would have to spend more time with the Semli and Nalghati families. In any case the lakes would be the first area to become accessible after the rains: the valleys of Semli and Nalghati would not open up for vehicles until weeks after we had been able to approach the lakes.

Early one morning, the day I was to leave, a huge storm came crashing through the park: thunder, lightning and torrents of rain. Visibility was down to little more than a metre. Within half an hour, as suddenly as it had come, the storm disappeared, leaving in its wake a blue sky and the early morning sun. What a transformation! The quality of light was special, the fragrance in the air magical. The leaves dripped

A sambar stag immersed in the waters of Rajbagh feeds on lotus leaves. Sambar are very fond of water plants and evade attack from crocodiles by kicking at them. Occasionally an adult sambar may fall prey to crocodiles, but this does not deter them from entering the water to feed. The sambar around the lakes have apparently adapted their feeding habits to include water plants, just as the tigers have evolved hunting techniques that enable them to prey on the deer in the water.

Ranthambore in the monsoon. A view from the fort reveals Jogi Mahal at the edge of Padam Talao, and Rajbagh in the distance. The forest has clothed itself with a lush green canopy.

with water and the forest glistened as if it had been cleansed. Torrents of water cascaded down the hillside and waterfalls sprouted from steep cliff faces and the edges of the fortress. These would be the last heavy showers before the rain wore off. It was time to leave for the station. As we turned a bend in the road that runs to Sawai Madhopur a tiger cut across our path. As it paused briefly to look at us, we realised that it was Noon. She ambled off towards the ravine where her cubs were born, disappearing into a profusion of green.

68

Growing Up

By the middle of October I was back in the folds of the forest canopy. Road gangs were still at work in the forest, and the vehicle tracks around the lakes were complete. Checking with the forest guards I found that tiger sightings had been irregular over the last weeks and none of the cubs had been seen. The forest was still green, the cover and undergrowth dense, the water well dispersed. I had brief glimpses of a few sambar and chital deer on the lakeside but they too were widely dispersed. Compared to the month of May, I felt I was in another forest, so sharp was the difference in colour during these two seasons. The roads leading to Semli and Nalghati were not complete. I spent the first week around the lakes in search of Noon and her cubs. There were several occasions when I heard scare calls of langurs and deer, but I never had a glimpse of the tiger. Even pugmark impressions on the tracks were difficult to find. The roads were still hard and it would take a few weeks for the soil to soften and reveal the impressions upon it.

Towards the end of the month the vehicle track into Semli and Nalghati was complete. This is a special moment if you happen to be one of the first to drive through it. After a break of nearly four months, it feels like your first drive into a forest. The animals have not seen or heard human beings or noisy vehicles for some time. They are jittery and flee at the slightest sound. It takes some time for them to adjust.

After several days of roaming around I found Laxmi sleeping quietly behind some rocks near the Semli water hole. I watched her for a while, scanning the area around for some signs of her cubs. Thirty minutes later there was a sound of an animal moving in the dense cover behind her. Laxmi looked up as one of her female cubs poked her head out of the cover. After four months the difference in size was remarkable. The cub was now ten months old and looked like a young tiger. After this long gap the cub was a bit shy and evasive. In minutes she was joined by her two siblings. They all looked well fed and fit. They soon reclined and slept. I was delighted to see them flourishing.

I decided to leave and drive fourteen kilometres into the Nalghati valley. On entering the valley I heard the barking of a troop of monkeys. Turning off the engine, I watched. Thirty metres to my right the grass started moving and a tiger emerged. It was Nalghati's male cub. He had the first signs of a ruff of hair around his cheeks. From some distance behind him the female cub poked out her head. She was smaller and shyer, but both cubs looked in excellent shape. They were eleven months old. Of the mother there was no sign.

It seemed to be my lucky day. The Nalghati valley was in shadow. In

69

the distance the sun struck the edge of the fort. I always try to get to the lakes at that time of the evening – they are better lit than the valleys. One of my favourite spots here is an incline between the first two lakes. At dusk, this is the point that evokes for me everything that I feel for Ranthambhore. Reaching it I turned the engine off. The sun was dipping behind a hill. The water of Padam Talao reflected this surreal light. The ramparts of the fort had taken on a strange glow as the sun vanished from the horizon. The grey partridge called endlessly until the crickets took over. Day was turning into night. Suddenly from Jogi Mahal a sambar bellowed in alarm. A troop of monkeys cackled and barked. The sambar continued its alarm call – a sure sign of a predator. I rushed towards the sounds and encountered Noon with two five-month-old cubs, one male and one female, walking along the edge of the lake. It was the first time I had set eyes on Noon's cubs. A strange emotion overcame me. I watched them for ten minutes, until they strode off into high grass. What a day! I had seen all the families, nine tigers in all.

It is at this age of five months that cubs start to roam around more freely with their mother. They are as big as medium-sized dogs and the tigress moves them over greater distances, her hunting range expanding considerably compared to the earlier months. The young ones learn and absorb the details of their mother's home range. They familiarise themselves with various landmarks, water holes and day shelters that provide security, and watch and observe the prey species on which their future survival will depend. Observing their mother stalking and killing is a critical lesson for their future development. The cubs are too young to help in hunting and tend to get in the way most of the time. During this period the tigress instils discipline by the occasional slap and a complex series of sounds that teach the cubs to avoid danger or just remain quiet while she is out hunting.

In 1977 I had a remarkable encounter with the tigress Padmini, who had four twelve-month-old cubs and was in the process of training them to hunt. It was a time when artificial baits were often set in order to catch glimpses of the nocturnal and evasive tiger. One night we found Padmini and her family, and instead of tethering a buffalo Fateh decided to turn one loose near the tigers. Padmini moved in like a flash, but instead of killing the animal she disabled it with a heavy blow to its hind leg. She then withdrew and sat some distance away. The injured buffalo limped around in front of the cubs. Cautiously, two cubs approached it, but the buffalo bravely lowered his head, adopting an aggressive posture, and the cubs fled to cover. Again the cubs tried to encircle the buffalo but the same thing happened. This continued for thirty minutes with Padmini watching carefully. Finally the dominant male cub leapt on the buffalo's hindquarters, bringing it down. A second cub joined him and after several clumsy movements the male

OPPOSITE:
Noon strolls at the edges of Rajbagh, a chital fawn dangling from her mouth. She has just killed the fawn and is carrying it to her cubs, well hidden in a bank of grass on the far side. This encounter was made possible because of a troop of langur monkeys: their cackle barking directed us to the tigress.

OVERLEAF:
After spending an hour watching her cubs tear apart and consume the fawn in tall grass, Noon leads them towards Padam Talao, the first lake. It is about ten o'clock on a late January morning. Suddenly she senses the presence of some deer off the track. The cubs dart off; Noon crouches a few metres away.

sank his canines into the neck. Both soon started to feed on the rump. After half an hour Padmini rose and a low growl sent the two cubs scampering off. Now she tried to nudge the other two as if to say, 'Come on, it's your turn.' Not only were the cubs learning to hunt, but the mother was ensuring they all had an equal share of the food.

In the 1970s artificial baiting for tigers was a regular occurrence in most parks in India. It was the only way to observe and document tigers. In fact the first serious book on the tiger by the American zoologist George Schaller was based mainly on records over tethered baits. By 1980 baiting was banned in Project Tiger reserves. Tiger populations had increased and they could be observed without being lured by bait. I am against baiting as it prevents any truly natural documentation of the tiger. Its only use today might be in locating and identifying man-eating tigers.

Late one afternoon towards the end of November, I watched a chital doe which had just given birth to a fawn near Rajbagh. The fawn was on the ground making frantic efforts to rise. The placenta fell to the ground

The next moment, a sambar alarm calls from the direction in which the cubs disappeared. There is a rustle of feet and Noon leaps into the forest. We find her choking an adult sambar hind. She has a perfect grip on the throat, which she holds for a few minutes. The sambar is not quite dead; one of its legs twitches.

The cubs rush up to watch. This is how they will learn the art of hunting. In fact, they have helped Noon by forcing the sambar towards the forest track. The male cub rests his paw, very tentatively, on the sambar's flank.

and the doe quickly ate it. A newborn fawn is helpless and could easily fall victim to a jackal, hyena, leopard, or tiger. But there was no sign of a predator. The mother licked her young, prodding it with her head to encourage it to its feet. The fawn responded, rising shakily on its hind legs and then falling again. Soon it managed to stand and the doe nuzzled it. It tried desperately to search for milk. After much nosing around it found the teat. Within minutes the helpless fawn was transformed as if a surge of life had entered it. The chital doe walked off some metres away and the fawn tottered behind. From my right a burst of alarm calls warned of impending danger. Noon had appeared and immediately spotted mother and fawn. The fawn was clumsily moving around. The doe was frozen: it hadn't yet seen the tiger. Noon crouched low, her muscles bunched up. Slowly and stealthily she crept forward, moving from cover of bush and grass. About twenty metres separated the doe from the tigress. The doe finally spotted the tigress and turned to flee. The fawn, caught unawares, tried to follow but Noon raced in and pinioned the fawn in her paws. Gripping the fawn by the neck she took off towards a bank of grass, her prey dangling from her mouth. As she approached, her male cub rushed out, grabbed the fawn from her, and disappeared into the grass to feed. Noon and her female cub waited on the sidelines. The male cub in all these families seemed to assert his prerogative to eat first, and only after he was satisfied did the other cubs follow.

Interestingly, the female cub of the Semli family was the most confident in her attitude to human observers. Unlike her siblings, she approached close to the jeeps and never shied away. But within the family group the male tiger always asserted his rights over his siblings, especially in the eating hierarchy. The mother would sometimes intervene to ensure that the meat was shared.

By December 1986 we were in regular touch with all the families. All three mothers were spending most of their time in search of prey. They also had a number of regular resting places, strategically placed near water holes and on the routes used by deer and other species. Here they would sit and sleep, ever alert to the slightest sound or movement. The

Noon's male cub scaling a tree in the thick den in which he spent the first few months of his life: Noon moved them here when they were only a few weeks old after they were disturbed by road workers. All the cubs we observed used their original dens as day shelters.

Noon's eight month old male cub cuddles her at the edge of some grass. Such bouts of nuzzling and cuddling increase the cubs' confidence as they grow up. Even at this age they enjoy being suckled by their mother, though their size and sharp teeth are a deterrent and Noon seldom obliges.

cubs remained asleep wherever the tigress chose to leave them. But even when the tiger sleeps, its senses monitor the area around and it has the ability to attack suddenly from a sleeping position, and kill. I remember once watching Noon sleeping in a high bank of grass with only half an ear visible. A langur monkey walked by some ten metres away towards a tract of water. As it passed the sleeping tigress she was up and in two leaps had grabbed it between her paws before choking it with her canines. This is the only time I have seen a tiger killing a langur in the wild.

Individual tigresses vary a great deal in their choice of resting places. Some choose dense cover, others lie out amidst a few rocks or a small bush. They manage a perfection in camouflage, using the slightest available cover. While resting, tigers spend much of their time in the ritual of grooming. The tiger's rough tongue works over the paws, chest and every part of the body it manages to reach. Most of the time tigers conserve their energies for hunting.

At the beginning of 1987 Noon's cubs were seven months old and were frequently visible around the lakes. They also focused their activities around the spot where Noon had taken them soon after their birth. This area was thick and inaccessible and we would often lose sight of them, until one day Fateh and his genius managed to take the jeep into the area. We had followed the family and found the male cub perched high up on a tree. Noon sat below and the female cub was trying in vain to clamber up to join her brother, who kept pushing her down. Soon the cubs abandoned this game and snuggled up to their mother. She licked both of them, they rubbed their cheeks and flanks against her. One of the cubs jumped over her, another caught her tail. She closed her canines gently and affectionately over one of the cubs' head and rolled over on her back as the cubs stretched out on her belly. The cubs then chased each other around leaping up on their hind legs. Wrestling and gentle sparring not only gives the cubs practice in the effective use of their limbs, it also reinforces vital bonds between the family.

During the early part of 1987 we had several memorable encounters with Noon and her cubs. One day late in January we went off into a bitingly cold morning to look for them. The chill factor in an open jeep in this season is 0°C. We stopped near Rajbagh and the barking of the langur monkey from the side of the lake spurred us on. The sun was just rising over the hill. Amidst a cacophony of chital, sambar and langur calls we arrived at one corner to find Noon walking nonchalantly with a chital fawn swinging in her mouth.

Noon walks along the shore of the lake. A few peahens take flight. She is heading for a bank of high grass. Suddenly two peacocks fly out of the grass closely followed by two racing cubs. The male, in the lead, grabs the fawn and darts back to a clump of grass. Noon licks her female cub, and they both recline at the edge of the grass. The male polishes off most of the carcass but towards the end Noon interrupts him. He snarls at her but she ignores him and picks up the remnants. The male cub moves away. The female cub joins her mother and they chew on the bits and pieces the male cub has left. An hour has gone by and soon mother and cubs leave the grass, walking across the edges of the lake towards Padam Talao. The cubs jump and chase each other as they walk around the lake. One charges into Noon and she snarls in annoyance. All three have now reached the edge of the first lake. The cubs turn a corner and disappear around the edge of the lake. Noon walks in front of us on the vehicle track. Two sambar alarms blast the silence near the cubs. They have been seen. Noon is now completely alert and darts forward on the track, realising that the sambar is caught between the

OPPOSITE:
Noon's cub sits comfortably in a tree below the walls of the fort, apparently enjoying being able to survey the scene below. Langur monkeys nearby are not used to seeing a tiger in a tree and flee with high-pitched shrieks.

OVERLEAF:
One of Noon's cubs, aged nine months, explores the parapet of a deserted mosque, one of Noon's day shelters.

track and her cubs. The cubs are assisting her unintentionally. There is a thud of hooves and a noise in the undergrowth. Noon has settled down on her belly, frozen to the ground at a point where a narrow animal path leads out from the edge of the lake. She has judged the exit point exactly. A large rock hides her. In a flash she leaps into the forest and is out of sight. We hear a grunt. Moving ahead, we find her a few metres off the track, in the throes of killing an adult sambar hind. She has a perfect killing grip on the throat. The sambar's legs twitch in vain: the grip is firm. The cubs approach cautiously and watch her intently. The male cub moves to the carcass but a flicker from the sambar's hind leg forces it to retreat. In minutes the sambar is dead. The male cub rests his forepaw on the rump, while Noon still holds her grip and the female cub stands near her mother. Noon drags the carcass away to where a thick bush makes visibility difficult. The cubs jump all over the sambar and their mother. A kill of this size feeds mother and cubs for three days.

Noon's cubs had unintentionally helped their mother kill the sambar. Slowly, as the cubs grew, this process became more planned. The Semli cubs, now thirteen months old, were already working with their mother when she hunted. Not yet able to kill for themselves, they would take up three different positions and try to scare the deer in the direction of their mother. With four tigers circling an area the prey would invariably panic and the mother's chances of success seemed better.

In the middle of February that year I had what I consider to be my most exciting time ever with tigers. I had returned from the morning drive and had a brief glimpse of Noon and her cubs as they moved towards a dense area below the walls of the fort. I was happily eating breakfast when a sambar alarm called twice. I left everything, grabbed the closest camera and, with Fateh's son, jumped into my jeep. As we came to the clearing between the two lakes we found Noon and her cubs moving across towards Rajbagh. She had suddenly changed her mind about her day shelter. It was 10.30 in the morning. The setting was perfect as the three tigers cut across the first lake, with the backdrop of the fort. Soon they passed an old ruin which must have been the entrance to a mosque in times gone by. Now overgrown by grass and shrubs, it was one of Noon's regular day shelters. She passed by, but her male cub, curious and frisky, decided to investigate and climbed up the steps to a parapet where he posed against the minarets. A splendid sight. He watched us for a while before jumping down to follow Noon. A sambar in the distance bellowed in alarm, a peacock took flight, shrieking as the family moved towards Mori, a secluded corner of the

second lake. They quenched their thirst around a small pool of water. One of the cubs jumped right over it and they slowly walked away and out of sight. The few sambar calls at breakfast had been responsible for a fruitful encounter and I felt cheerful as I turned the jeep to head back to base.

Suddenly from where the tigers had disappeared comes one of the largest sambar stags I have ever seen, galloping out, closely pursued by Noon. My mouth falls open. I cannot believe it. Does Noon expect to kill such a large stag in a chase over open ground? Stag and tigress are out of sight some thirty metres ahead. Fumbling with the starter of the jeep I move ahead, heart pounding. A couple of metres from the vehicle track in the clearing the sambar stag stands motionless. Noon clings on to the side of its neck. Her canines have a grip, but they are nowhere near the throat. Both tiger and sambar are frozen in this position, staring at each other. There is not a sound or a movement. It is a scene I never expected to see in my life. Goverdhan, Fateh's son, wakes me from my daze: 'Come on, use your camera, we will never see this again.' My revery broken, I swing into action, cursing myself in the process. In the rush of departure I simply picked up the nearest camera which has only an 85 mm lens, and no more than twenty shots left; I have no more film on me. Such is jungle life sometimes. I take a few quick pictures, not sure how steady my hands are in the excitement of the moment. Goverdhan warns me to be careful. Sambar and tiger are still locked together. I decide to change position and move up to within three metres of them. They are not in the least bothered by our presence, too involved in their own struggle. I am so close that I feel I could touch them. I choose my shots carefully so as not to finish the film too soon. Noon seems unwilling to shift her grip, which might allow the sambar to escape. A few parakeets fly overhead, some green pigeons chatter in a tree nearby as tiger and sambar remain locked together.

In a few minutes the sambar, with a great heave of his neck, shrugs the tigress off but in a flash she attacks his forelegs in an effort to break them. The stag jerks away, but Noon goes again for the neck, rising on her haunches with one paw on his shoulder for leverage. But in vain. The sambar swivels around and Noon now attacks the belly. With much struggling in the region of the belly and hind legs, she succeeds and the sambar finds itself in a sitting position while the

Noon's female cub jumps across a pool of water. At this moment the family disappeared. The forest was silent. Then a huge sambar stag raced across our path, hotly pursued by Noon. We followed.

We found tiger and sambar locked together, motionless. They remained like this for several minutes. Noon had grabbed the sambar by the back of the neck, but her canines had been unable to find a killing grip. The sambar is battle scarred, with patches of hair missing from his flank. It is near the end of the rutting season and this stag must have clashed with others in the last few months. Now the clash is a matter of life and death. Notice how the sambar keeps his tail raised in alarm.

Noon curves her body, using all her strength and leverage to force the sambar's head down and break the deadlock. Notice the power of her rear flanks as she applies pressure on the sambar, who must weigh about 300 kg.

The stag has shaken off Noon's grip, but Noon has managed to grasp him at the back of the head. She is using all her strength, balancing on her hind legs, her forelegs pressed against the sambar's shoulder. If she can topple him to the ground, her task will become easier. She desperately keeps away from the antlers and her pressure on the neck forces the sambar's hind legs off the ground. They are locked in a fierce struggle.

They swivel around. Noon is forced down and the stag lowers his antlers to protect himself. Noon tries to grip the sambar below the ear and at the same time attempts to muzzle him with her right paw. The sambar's left foreleg is off the ground and pressing against Noon's face. His tail is still upright!

The struggle continues – Noon clings on as the sambar stag swivels around. She is now frantic to get him down and prevent him escaping. She finds herself in the strangest position, completely underneath the sambar's body. Her strong right paw now grips his neck, claws extended for a better hold. Her head is somewhere near his chest and the sambar's right foreleg is against the tiger's shoulder.

The sambar, using all his strength, raises his head and shrugs Noon off. She is forced to attack his left hind leg, which she grasps between her paws and attempts to bite. This is her last opportunity to break his legs. Notice her teeth marks on the right hind leg.

Noon twists and bites at the left hind leg, forcing the sambar to topple. His forelegs crash down and his head rests on the ground. Notice how the bulk strength of the tiger is combined with the leverage gained as she grips the ground with the claws of her right hind leg extended.

With a great heave the stag rises from the ground and attempts to escape. Noon desperately attacks from the rear, her tail raised for balance and her canines sunk into the sambar's hind leg.

Noon succeeds and the sambar comes crashing down. Noon hangs on to the hind leg for dear life. At this moment her nine month old male cub appears from the grass from where he has been watching the encounter, observing the fine art of hunting. He seems to think that his mother has won the battle, and approaches cautiously. But the stag suddenly frees his hind legs and dashes off unsteadily towards the waters of Rajbagh. The male cub flees. Noon tries to pursue the stag, but the efforts of the past minutes have been too exhausting. The sambar escapes.

tigress takes a firm grip on one of its hind legs. My film is slowly running out. Suddenly Noon's male cub appears and stands motionless observing the encounter. Noon and sambar are again frozen in their position. The cub inches closer, perhaps sensing victory. Noon yanks at the hind leg, opening the skin and trying desperately to break it. This is the only way she will prevent the stag from escaping, as her grip is not a fatal one. I am totally mesmerised. The cub must be learning a lot from watching the combat.

Suddenly, the sambar, utilising every ounce of his strength, shakes Noon off, stands and runs. The cub flees in fear, and an exhausted Noon tries to chase the sambar. The sambar, with a burst of adrenalin, escapes in the direction from which he has come, towards the edge of Rajbagh. Noon lopes after him, but hasn't the energy to sustain any speed. Her cubs come around as if egging her on but she snarls at them in irritation. The cubs run ahead of her, following the sambar to the water's edge. The stag alarm calls for the first time, a strange dull and hollow sound as if his vocal chords have been damaged in the attack. Seeing the approaching tigers he wades into the lake. Noon and her cubs now watch anxiously from the shore. The stag has great difficulty moving through the water. He stumbles forward and finds himself in a deep patch; he is forced to swim and nearly drowns. His head bobs up and down, his limbs move frantically as he struggles to reach the far bank. The tigers follow along the shore but Noon soon gives up and reclines at the edge, exhausted and panting. Her tongue is cut and bleeding. Her cubs jump around her but she snarls at them and they lie down to rest under the shade of a bush.

The stag limps towards the shore and stands motionless for many minutes in the shallow water. Noon watches for a bit but then decides against pursuing her quarry and walks away into the dense cover of Mori to shelter. Her cubs follow. The sambar slowly hobbles out of the water on to a bank of grass. His right foreleg looks twisted and broken; patches of skin have been raked and a bloody injury swells on the side of his neck. How he had found the strength to escape I can't fathom. Now this magnificent stag is a sorry sight.

It was 12.10 in the afternoon. Goverdhan and I returned to Jogi Mahal, elated by what we had seen. I spent most of the evening chattering away to Fateh about this incredible encounter. I realised that there would not have been much to see or photograph if the tigress had taken

OPPOSITE
The Bakaula tigress, whose home range adjoins Laxmi's, with whom she shares the Bakaula male's territory. When this picture was taken, she had two cubs, but they were seldom seen. She was much more elusive than Laxmi. Here she sits perfectly camouflaged amidst the low-lying leaves of a tree – an ideal spot to rest during the day in anticipation of a deer or antelope that might pass by.

Nalghati's female cub, aged fifteen months, reclining on the branch of a tree. The thick growth of leaves provides shade. This is the oldest cub we saw in a tree – after about fifteen months they become too heavy and bulky to clamber up successfully.

a grip on the stag's throat instead of the side of his neck: he would then have been nearly dead by the time we arrived on the scene. It was pure luck. My fingers remained crossed for a long time till the film was processed. The stag remained rooted to the same area for many days, his wounds worsening slowly. Noon never went back to find him. The following day she killed another stag on the plateau above. In a few weeks the stag died at the edge of the lake and was consumed by crocodiles. Sad as it may seem, this is the way of the forest.

It was also in the course of this month that I saw one of the most depressing sights I had ever seen in the forest. I had just returned from the Semli valley after three enjoyable hours of observation with the family. Minutes later Fateh arrived and asked me to come and look into his jeep. I was shocked. Three dead cubs lay piled up in the back. It was an emotional moment. Spending long hours with three cubs and then finding three dead ones leaves one speechless.

The story unfolded. The cubs had been found dead in an adjoining tract of forest a few kilometres away from the park. It was the Man Singh Sanctuary, an area encroached by graziers and cattle. It is also an area where an endless series of stone quarries has totally destroyed some of the finest stretches of Dhok forest. These are examples of man's mindless exploitation of nature for temporary gains.

Within this disturbed sanctuary a tigress had given birth to three cubs and they had all survived till the age of seven months, a time when a cub's appetite increases rapidly and regular meat is essential. I was convinced that the mother had been forced to kill them as she was unable to feed them. The next morning an autopsy revealed not a sign of food in the stomachs or intestine. All the cubs had been choked to death by a grip on their nape and throat. Ground tracks in the area indicated the mother's marks but no signs of a struggle. They must have rushed up to her, restless with hunger, moaning and wailing for food. While they nuzzled her she had used her canines, crushing the first cervical vertebra and the occipital segment of the cranium. They died at a distance of some thirty metres from each other. What a terrifying time it must have been. But for a mother in these circumstances this is the only way to end the misery of the cub. It also enables tigers to maintain some balance, especially when there is a shortage of prey. Man degrades forest tracts and this is the result. I tossed and turned that night, itching to get back to the living cubs the next morning.

We were into early March and the Semli cubs were fourteen months old, the Nalghati cubs fifteen months. During the last couple of months there had been a considerable widening of the area that both tigresses and their cubs had been using. The Semli family was on the periphery of Lakarda, and the Nalghati family, near Phutakot, both several kilometres from their earlier dens. This increased mobility brought the cubs into contact with more prey and unexplored areas. They were now hunting with their mother, more often assisting in a three-pronged attack to force the prey towards her. This is also an age when the physical closeness between the cubs begins to lessen, especially when their mother is absent. They no longer sleep cuddled up together, heads on flanks and paws on heads, as they used to; they keep more of a distance. They are growing up.

HERE AND OVERLEAF:
Noon's nine month old cubs playing. When the mother is away hunting, the cubs remain close to the spot where they have been left. At this age they explore only the immediately surrounding area and generally feel quite insecure in their mother's absence.

Playing and cuddling reasserts close physical bonds between the siblings. This also assists them in the use of their forelegs, which will later play a critical role in hunting.

Noon snarls at her male cub, now eleven months old, as the family comes to the edge of Padam Talao to cool off on a hot summer's day. These snarls, growls and coughs are the tiger's language and Noon uses them to instil discipline into the cubs: this is vital for their development and for the success of Noon's predatory activity; it also teaches them when to move and when to be motionless, laying the foundation for their hunting techniques.

Laxmi's male cub watches a pair of Indian gazelles or chinkaras, one of the most dainty and elegant antelopes to be found in Ranthambhore's forests. They are fast and agile, and there is only one recorded case of a tiger killing them. At this age – fifteen months – the cubs start to hunt on their own, and even manage sometimes to kill small creatures such as hares, fawns and peacocks.

Physical bonds within the family no longer play such a critical part in the cubs' lives. The tiger is a solitary predator and this distancing between the siblings is the first indication of the independence from the family unit they will gradually develop.

One warm day in March I arrived at the Semli water hole to find the three cubs resting in the cool of the undergrowth. The female cub moved towards us as we arrived, in her normal way, walking past very close to the jeep. There was no sign of Laxmi. The cubs lazed around for nearly an hour and at four o'clock one of them suddenly became alert. It darted off to the far side, followed by its siblings. The forest exploded with the sound of purring as the cubs exhaled in great bursts, probably indicating joy. We followed to find the cubs rubbing their flanks against Laxmi. All four tigers purred incessantly, as if orchestrated, as the cubs licked, nuzzled and cuddled their mother. Purring probably starts around the age of ten to twelve months. Certainly I have not heard younger cubs purring. This is how the cubs greet their mother on her return after a long stretch of being away.

The purring continues for nearly ten minutes, as all four tigers walk towards us. The cubs rub their bodies against Laxmi, expressing their delight at seeing her. They move to a water hole and quench their thirst, then Laxmi moves some twenty metres away to rest in the shade of a tree. The cubs return to their original positions. It is nearly five in the evening and we decide to watch from a distance, hoping that some deer will soon come to the water hole to quench their thirst. At six o'clock a group of fourteen chital emerge from the cover of the forest and cautiously approach the water. Laxmi is suddenly alert, watching intently. The deer have not seen her or the cubs. The cubs lie frozen, knowing the slightest movement will give the game away. Most of the deer have their tails up. They are suspicious, but they need water. Slowly, step by step, they approach. They are now between the mother and her cubs. A perfect situation for Laxmi. She crouches, moves forward some three metres on her belly as if gliding along the ground. Then one chital alarm call pierces through the evening. Laxmi moves in a flash, her cubs sprint from the far side and in the panic and confusion of the moment a fawn gets separated and flees towards Laxmi. Laxmi pinions it between her paws and grabs the back of its neck. The fawn squeaks and dies. A stork-billed kingfisher flies away from its perch, its blue wings glinting in the late evening light. Picking up the fawn, Laxmi carries it some metres away. Her cubs move in, hoping to feast on a few morsels. Laxmi

Noon's cubs, aged twelve months. Noon's impatience forces her female cub into a submissive posture.

OVERLEAF, LEFT:
Noon's male cub, aged fourteen months, on an old wall below the ramparts of the fort. This is one of several entrances that protected the fort from opposing armies in the past. The first rains have transformed the forest to a deep green.

OVERLEAF, RIGHT:
Laxmi's thirteen and a half month old cub precariously balanced on a tree. The cubs are growing rapidly and climbing up and down trees is not so easy. This female cub suddenly decided to move towards the only tree in an area of open grassland and clambered up it: an extraordinary sight.

drops the fawn to the ground and settles on it, covering the tiny carcass with her paws. She turns and snarls viciously at the approaching cubs. One of the female cubs moves off but the male and the other female settle down to face their mother a metre away. Both cubs start a low-pitched moaning sound, which I have never heard before. It soon turns into a wail as if they were begging for the carcass. Laxmi snarls and coughs sharply at them. The male cub rises and moves towards her but she growls, picks up the carcass and settles down again some three metres ahead, the fawn between her

Laxmi with her three cubs cuddled up in the centre of a vehicle track. The male cub rests near his mother's forelegs and swats the female cub on the forehead with his paw. The cubs are just beginning to assert their independence from each other and from their mother.

Laxmi licks her female cub. The male cub strides forward to share his mother's attentions. They have just eaten a chital, and their bellies are bulging. It is amazing how much bigger the cubs look after a large meal.

paws. All three cubs settle down around her, moaning continuously. She snarls back and this continues for fifteen minutes. Suddenly two of her cubs 'cannonball' into her and all three tigers go rolling over in a flurry of activity, but the male cub snatches the carcass expertly and rushes away with it followed by one of his sisters. Laxmi sits unconcerned and proceeds to groom herself. The male will not tolerate his siblings on the carcass and they return to Laxmi. They watch the male cub eating. They wait patiently for 45 minutes until the fawn has been consumed. Then, they all move off. I

Laxmi relaxes in the foreground, her cubs rest on a ledge of a cliff face. The two females pat one another; the male, on the right, looks unconcerned. This is a typical family scene with all the tigers relaxed and in close physical proximity. They have just eaten a sambar hind and their bellies are heavy.

Laxmi rests near the carcass of a chital stag she killed the day before. Remaining close to a kill is the only way to ensure that scavenging birds don't make off with scraps. Some tigers keep a certain distance, but this forces them repeatedly to attack the tree pies or crows that come near the kill. Laxmi, unlike Kublai or the Bakaula male, is a slow eater and in the course of the night has only eaten the chital's hind quarters. Tigers vary enormously in eating habits from individual to individual.

have found that when the prey is tiny, the dominant cub asserts his right to eat most of it. He shares only when the kill is large.

It is around the age of about sixteen months that the first detachment in the relationships between the cubs occur. This probably assists them in getting accustomed to their future solitary existence.

By April the first aggressive interactions had begun between the Semli cubs, especially the females. When Laxmi was absent the females circled each other with low growls and when they were close to each

other, they would rear up on their hind legs, snarling viciously, and sometimes mock boxing. They seemed to be asserting their dominance and the smaller female tended to submit by rolling on her back. The male cub and the larger female spent more time together. They seemed closer. The smaller female tended to be left out except when Laxmi was around. She was her mother's favourite. The cubs' play was now rougher as they chased each other over long distances, crashing into one another and leaping at each other high in the air. They were young tigers now, beginning to assert their individual characteristics.

In the last few months the resident males had continued to interact

HERE AND OVERLEAF:
Laxmi's cubs play together. They are now seventeen months old and the play is more aggressive. The male cub dominates his sister as he swats her, then the female cub lands on his back and they end up in a heap. Laxmi turns her head to watch.

Laxmi's female cubs, aged seventeen months, in a mock fight for dominance. The contests are accompanied by ferocious snarls, growls and coughs but neither tiger actually harms the other. These bouts help prepare the young tigers for their quest for a home range of their own – the tests of strength are vital in the tiger's development.

with the families and their pugmarks had been found in the vicinity. In early May, Fateh found Kublai, the Nalghati tigress and her two sixteen month old cubs together around a sambar kill. Even at that age the cubs had no fear of the male. One day, towards the end of May, I found Kublai with Noon and her twelve month old cubs all sitting in a clearing. Soon Noon moved off with her cubs and Kublai retreated to dense cover for the day. So the resident males continued to remain in touch with the families in their area without any conflict.

It was at this time that the Bakaula tigress was also found with two eight month old cubs. We only caught a quick glimpse before they rushed off. The Bakaula tigress was very elusive and the second in the resident Bakaula male's range to be seen with cubs, after Laxmi. Soon afterwards the Basandhra tigress was seen with two cubs about the same size as Noon's. Her range met Noon's at one corner, the Nalghati tigress's at another, and parts of the fringes of the forest on the far side.

The resident male of her area was unknown. We had a few glimpses of this family but they were more evasive than the rest. Still, we had recorded five tigresses with cubs of different sizes.

The month of June was hot, and the lakes were shallow, rapidly drying up. Water was scarce. The shortage of water was greater than in previous years. The cubs were seen regularly around water holes, cooling off in the blistering heat. The forest was preparing for another monsoon. It would close up again for several months and in October 1987, the Semli and Nalghati cubs would be sub-adults. A new phase in their lives would start.

My last sight of tigers that season was late one evening in June when I found all three Semli cubs lazing around the only water hole in the area, without Laxmi. Quite suddenly a sambar hind appeared from the rear with two young ones. The three tigers quickly separated and from three different positions attacked this group. Tigers and sambars all fled from

Laxmi's male cub explores the entrance to an old hunting tower where in times gone by human predators must have sat in wait for the tiger. Now deserted and ruined, it is part of Laxmi's home range.

Laxmi snarls at her sixteen month old cub as it nuzzles her. The cubs compete constantly for their mother's attention, not giving her a moment's peace. If she is not out hunting, she is repeatedly cuddled and nuzzled. But she still shows complete devotion to her cubs.

sight. Moving the jeep around I discovered to my total surprise the male cub choking one of the deer with his canines. He was eighteen months old and it was the first successful kill I had seen with the three cubs working as a team. They had learnt the nuances of hunting that make the tiger such a powerful predator.

OVERLEAF, TOP LEFT:
Laxmi (left) and two of her three cubs at seventeen months. They are resting during the day close to the Semli water hole. At times like this all four tigers would suddenly burst out of the forest if an unsuspecting herd of deer was coming to drink.

OVERLEAF, BOTTOM LEFT:
Laxmi's male cub, aged eighteen months, stretches towards the sky – a portrait of a fine young male.

OVERLEAF, RIGHT:
Laxmi with her nineteen month old cubs at the Semli water hole. The family cool themselves on a hot summer's evening.

Laxmi's two seventeen month old cubs relax late one evening at the edge of the Semli water hole. At this age the cubs look like young tigers.

Independence

By October of 1987 all the cubs had grown. The Nalghati cubs were 23 months, the Semli cubs 22 and Noon's cubs in their seventeenth month. The three months of the wet season had been critical in the development of the Semli and Nalghati families. The cubs were now sub-adults and were probably mature and independent enough to go their own ways. The rains that year had been poor. Though the forest was green, Padam Talao and Rajbagh were about half full and Malik Talao merely a pool of water. The contrast with previous years was striking. The failure of a good monsoon two years running would cause havoc in the area. Lack of rain means that crops fail, little income is generated for the farmer, necessary fodder is not available for cattle, and dried up wells create a severe water shortage. The pressures on a forest mount, as water is better conserved in the natural reservoirs of a forest, thick and shaded against the heat of the sun. Compared with the outside world, the forest offers many more possibilities for fodder, leaf litter and other nutrients that cattle can survive on. So man and his livestock are desperate to rush in.

Every year the vehicle tracks in Ranthambhore are washed away by the rain, and road gangs are busy after September relinking the different areas in the forest. Sometimes late rain causes this work to stretch on to the end of October. That October the roads to Semli and Nalghati were not ready and I could not trace the cubs. But late one evening around Malik Talao a burst of chital calls indicated the presence of Noon and soon we found her in a clump of grass. Without warning she leapt forwards and there was a squeak. She appeared from the grass carrying a chital fawn and moved across to another bank of grass where both her cubs darted towards her, the male snatching the fawn. But the cubs were both large and the female cub also gripped the carcass; for a while both cubs remained frozen, holding on to either end of the fawn. Then began a frantic tug of war as the little fawn was rocked from side to side. Noon reclined a distance away as the cubs fought over their right to eat. Amidst several growls and snarls the male finally won the bout and disappeared to eat on his own. When the cubs are this age, the mother will provide a regular supply of food for them, but for the rest of the time the cubs are left on their own, sometimes for as long as a couple of days.

The cubs are no longer rooted to a spot. They wander around their mother's range, keeping in touch with her movements through scent and the occasional sound. The cubs are forced to fend for themselves and attempt their first stalks for prey. They succeed sometimes with

Nalghati's male cub strikes a pose, clutching on to a large rock with his forelegs. Our jeep was stranded at this spot and both cubs watched us from the rocks for an hour until another jeep came to help us. At eighteen months the Nalghati cubs were often left for a day, or even two, by their mother and for the first time they were fending for themselves. The male would take charge and even attempt, with his sister, successful attacks on chital.

Noon's cub leaps off the ground and streaks towards its mother at the edge of the lake.

peafowl, monkeys and the fawns of various deer. It is a critical time in their lives when their ability to survive is put on test. Has the mother's training been efficient and effective?

It was only sometime in November that we rediscovered the Semli family. We found the small and most curious female cub spending much of her time in the Lakarda valley, within her mother's range. She seemed to have separated from both mother and siblings. The male and the larger female cub, now adult tiger size, were found together in the Semli valley. Sometimes they were separated by several hundred metres, but they were still in the same vicinity. On one occasion Laxmi arrived with the smaller cub and all four spent the evening together. We found evidence that their movements overlapped and occasionally they would share food, but Laxmi spent most of the time on her own, as did her small cub, although the other two chose to stay together. All the cubs had been seen with their own kills, so we knew they were able to hunt and survive independently.

The months of November and December were difficult for Ranthambhore and its inmates. Successive periods of drought had created tremendous pressure on the natural fodder and water that remained within the park. Thousands of cattle and their graziers repeatedly entered the park in an endless quest for grazing lands and timber for

A portrait of Noon's male cub, aged 24 months, as he reclines on a stretch of black rock.

fuel. During this period innumerable livestock fell to the predators of the park. This included camels, which tigers relish given the opportunity. In Kachida valley two leopards killed a cow and fed on it for a day; by the next morning a tigress had appropriated the carcass. This invasion created unnatural conditions in which there was more interaction between the predators and livestock. This meant that the wild ungulates and the predators would both suffer during the course of the year, because of the damage done to the forest. Also, graziers tend to carry poison and when an animal is killed they poison the carcass. The predators of Ranthambhore always remain around their kills and this could have fatal consequences. In fact late in December, just near the main entrance to the park, a twenty-month-old tiger was found, apparently poisoned. He had been eating a buffalo that had entered the park the day before. It was probably one of the Basandhra tigress's cubs.

Fateh and I were extremely concerned about the situation but Fateh was limited to giving advice. A few months earlier, after twenty years of looking after tigers, he had been transferred to another area where there were no tigers. Choosing to stay in Ranthambhore, he was now on extended leave. We spent many hours discussing the problem of livestock with the new director of the park: Fateh's experience was extremely helpful and by early 1988 more effort was being made to

Noon's cubs jump towards each other in a test of strength while Noon lies nonchalantly in the foreground. Notice the flexibility of the paws as the cubs attempt to swat each other.

keep livestock out of the park – and it was proving effective.

It was during January that we noticed Noon's male cub developing a much greater degree of independence from both his mother and his sister. He could be found on his own, strolling around the area of the lakes, though if Noon happened to kill, then suddenly the whole family came together to feast. Late that month we were fortunate enough to witness a rare encounter between the tigers. Early one morning while driving through the gentle layers of mist around the lakes, we found an Egyptian vulture circling a bank of high grass around Malik Talao. A few crows flew noisily around a patch in the grass. A tree pie darted around, indicating a precise spot. The grass was too high for us to see anything and we decided to take the jeep through. A few metres in, we found Noon resting and both her cubs tearing at the hindquarters of a large sambar stag. The male cub had his own piece and the female ate from the carcass. The stag had probably been killed the previous evening. We had been watching the tigers for about half an hour when suddenly, from a long way off, came the persistent alarm calls of a sambar. So frequent were they that it seemed to confirm that yet another tiger was in the area. We decided to investigate and from the rise of a hill we saw, padding along the vehicle track, a very large male tiger. I didn't recognise him: he seemed to be a transient male. At a junction between various tracks he sniffed the ground and the bark of a tree repeatedly, and chose to move towards the bank of high grass. Maybe he had picked up Noon's scent from the previous evening. Now sniffing the air he carefully circled the grass and then walked through it. Naturalists

OPPOSITE TOP:
One of Noon's cubs watches a pair of peacocks through the cover of tall grass. Both young and adult tigers kill and eat peacocks, and cubs learn their first lessons in hunting by stalking them.

OPPOSITE BOTTOM AND BELOW:
Noon in full flight after a peacock, with her cubs just behind. One of the cubs appears a little tentative, but Noon leads the attack, forcing her cubs to follow.

RIGHT:
A transient male hangs his tongue out in the gesture of 'flehmen' after sniffing the spray marking of Noon and her cubs. The spray is fresh and Noon and the cubs are in the bank of high grass. Instead of acting as a deterrent, the scent attracts this big male; he approaches and Noon cautiously moves towards him.

BELOW:
They clash. Rearing up on their hind legs they attempt to box each other with their paws in an assertion of dominance. The transient male has detected the scent of a kill and is determined to exercise his power to annex the carcass.

OPPOSITE:
Noon defends herself gallantly, landing a left punch to the tiger's face. But her efforts are in vain. The male appropriates the carcass. Noon's male cub has rushed off to safety. Transient males can be a threat to cubs and potentially competitive territorially.

have often claimed that a tiger's sense of smell is slight and hardly put to use, but I have repeatedly seen tigers sniffing their way along in their efforts to unravel some of the secrets a forest might hold.

The male tiger has reached the far side of the grass, thirty metres from Noon's family, and at the edge of the grass he flops down and appears to go to sleep. By this time Noon is carefully inching her way out of the long grass towards the male, her eyes peering anxiously in an effort to scan the area. She suspects possible danger but the grass is too tall for her to pinpoint the position of the intruder. She remains frozen for some minutes, looking carefully in the general direction of the male tiger. Suddenly the male flicks his tail, a few blades of grass move and Noon has located her quarry. Completely alert and tense, she starts to stalk towards him. It takes her fifteen minutes to move thirty metres. She moves so gently that you cannot hear the sound of her weight on dry grass. Head lowered, muscles bunched up near her shoulders, she comes to a halt a couple of metres from the male tiger. Now she remains frozen, watching him, clearly realising his potential threat. She looks as if she will attack. The male has his eyes closed. I wonder if he is playing a game. Cautiously Noon takes another step forward and suddenly the male swivels around, confronting her with a vicious growl, and in a flash both tigers rear up on their hind legs, literally standing to face one another. They keep their balance for a bit as they gently try and slap each other, then lower themselves with the most blood-curdling growls. They rise on their hind legs three times in this way before sitting down to face each other. The forest goes silent.

Noon is soon up and quickly tries to return to her carcass. In the distance I see her male cub running away. The male tiger follows Noon. The female cub now leaves the grass and attempts to nuzzle the male but he snarls and mother and daughter watch him as he enters the grass and appropriates the carcass. Noon follows him but as she approaches, she is met by a series of low growls. She retreats with her cub to settle down at the edge of the grass in the shade of a tree. There is no sign of the male cub. After a while the female cub attempts to enter the grass, approaching cautiously. She persists until she is within a metre of the male but his aggression soon forces her away.

Late in the afternoon the female cub is again attracted to the carcass. Despite much growling by the male she manages

Noon and her female cub with the remnants of the carcass the next morning. The transient male has gone, and mother and cub are left with the scraps.

Portrait of Noon's male cub.

ABOVE AND OPPOSITE:
Noon's female cub charges a scavenging tree pie from a chital kill, then lifts the remnants to carry them into thicker forest to feed.

to snatch one of the legs of the deer but in the process she receives a swipe on her foreleg which causes a small gash. Unconcerned, she continues to chew on what she has retrieved. Noon remains out of the fray and reclines outside the patch of grass. Late that evening a sounder of wild boar, attracted by the stench of the carcass, approach warily, see Noon, and trot off.

The next morning we found Noon and her female cub chewing on the many remnants of the carcass. The male tiger had left the area after eating his fill. There was still no sign of Noon's male cub. Noon chewed at the flesh between the antlers while her cub stripped the last meat from one of the forelegs. By eleven o'clock they had finished feeding and mother and cub moved out of Malik Talao into a network of ravines. I didn't see the male cub till three days later when he had joined his mother and sister on another sambar kill. He was spending more time on his own and had avoided possible conflict with the male tiger by preferring to slip away. It was the first time that we had seen interactions between a transient male and a resident tigress.

The Nalghati cubs were over two years old and though male and female cub were sometimes together there were few signs of the mother. Both cubs were able to kill, sometimes in tandem but also on

their own. Our study of them was over and we spent most of our time observing Noon and her offspring around the lakes.

At about five o'clock one evening in February, three of the larger crocodiles in Rajbagh attacked a medium-sized sambar hind in about a metre of water. Fateh watched this encounter unfold. One crocodile made desperate efforts to yank the hind leg, while another tried to grab the neck, amidst much turning and twisting of their bodies. The sambar was frozen, unable to move out of the water. Other deer around the lakes alarm called and within ten minutes the sambar was slowly sinking into the water, gaping wounds around its neck and rump. There was now a swirling mass of crocodiles around the sambar and it soon drowned amidst the onslaught. The crocodiles were having difficulty wrenching the carcass open to devour it. Suddenly Noon and her cubs appeared on the scene.

> The cubs sit on their haunches to watch while Noon circles the shore, moving towards the crocodiles. She stops to watch the activity for a few minutes and then enters the shallow water, slowly at first, a little tentative, gingerly picking her steps through the lake bed. Suddenly with a burst of speed she rushes straight for the crocodiles and the carcass. Snarling viciously she slaps at the water and the crocodiles are forced

Noon pounds the water with her paws, appropriating a sambar carcass from a dozen crocodiles feeding in the shallow waters of Rajbagh. Noon is the dominant scavenger of the lakes; her water-based predation enables her to compete successfully with the crocodiles for prey. She drags the carcass towards the shore and is joined by her nineteen month old cubs. Noon tries to drag the heavy carcass backwards up a bank of high grass. The cubs are anxious to help. One of them tugs at her tail, behaving more like a primate than a big cat.

OPPOSITE:
Noon's cubs, eighteen months old, follow their mother through thick forest, alert to the movements of some chital on the far side. The cubs now actively participate in hunting, sometimes even successfully.

LEFT:
Noon's male cub busily grappling with the remnants of a sambar carcass. He tugs at the neck, using his paw to keep a hold on the head. Every scrap of meat is consumed, even the little flesh around the head. The carcass is licked clean with an abrasive tongue.

Noon's male cub at 23 months, just after killing a young neelgai or great Indian antelope. This was the first time we saw him with his own kill. Noon's training has worked – he can now hunt and kill for himself, which is essential for his survival.

to retreat. Fateh estimates that there were nearly twenty crocodiles around the dead sambar. A large one still guards the floating carcass but Noon rushes at him and smacks her paw into the water with such force that the crocodile glides away. Quickly grabbing the carcass by the throat she starts to pull it out of the water. It requires a herculean effort. The cubs, who have been watching attentively from the shore, now race across towards their mother, meeting her just as she is about to reach dry land. She stops as the cubs nuzzle her and jump about the carcass. She then proceeds to drag it back on to dry land, moving in reverse. Her male cub grasps her tail as if to say, 'I'll pull you too' and then to Fateh's surprise the female cub also attempts to pull her brother's tail. This strange procession of tigers moves slowly to a bank of grass with the sambar, pausing every now and then to rest during this exhausting activity.

Noon's two year old cubs quench their thirst at the edge of the lake. A group of sambar graze in the background. It is a blazing summer day with the temperature at 46°C. Water holes have dried out rapidly under a scorching sun. This is the last patch of water left in Rajbagh. In this heat tigers — and all the other animals in the forest — are forced to remain close to water.

The water in the lakes was drying rapidly. For the first time in the history of the park, Padam Talao, the first lake, had been reduced to a large

pool of water. Deer, boar and antelope grazed on the dry bed of the lake. It would be completely dry by May. A few crocodiles remained in the pool, but most of them had migrated towards Rajbagh. Rajbagh was a larger, shallow tract of water but also drying rapidly. What would be the fate of these hundred crocodiles? Where would they go? There was too little water in the ravines for them to survive. There would be few fish for them to feed on. The whole ecology of the area around the lakes was undergoing a change. The lack of water might create a severe problem.

By early March Noon's male cub was turning into a lake expert, following in the footsteps of his mother. He was persistent in his attempts to charge deer from banks of high grass, sometimes even racing into the shallow water in the lake to attack his quarry. The female cub was more reticent. She would join her mother and brother after their attacks or charges.

Noon and the cubs frequented the area around Jogi Mahal. I remember a group of us were sitting around a fire one cold winter's night, in a courtyard surrounded by a wall. Between a few drinks and a lot of chatter I suddenly heard the grass rustling outside. I quietly left the

Noon's female cub walks under one of the largest banyan trees in India, near Jogi Mahal, the forest rest house. She also strolls around on her own, but her links with Noon are much closer than those of her brother.

group and looked over the wall; to my delight I found Noon standing below on a forest track. We looked at each other for a few seconds, then I turned and signalled to the group around the fire, who were now quite noisy. They thought I was mad as I waved my hands up and down. It took them a moment to realise what I was trying to say, but then, in silence, they crept over to the wall. Noon had been joined by her cubs. One of the group couldn't control herself and exclaimed loudly. Noon turned and coughed, moving off towards the kitchen, her cubs scampering ahead. I couldn't believe it when I suddenly saw one of the forest guards carrying our dinner on a tray, walking towards the male cub. Fateh yelled to him. I had visions of the dinner in a mess on the floor and a man scurrying away, but the guard kept his cool and, realising his predicament, turned and walked back to the kitchen. Noon and her cubs passed by.

The male cub spent most of his time around the rest house. Once he was calmly reclining in the evening around the area where the cars are parked. He had even walked through the kitchen towards a lower corridor of the building. Even though these tigers had never threatened a human being, this behaviour gave cause for concern. In fact Fateh and I felt responsible for the close proximity the tigers enjoyed with the jeeps. Our fingers are crossed to this day that no untoward incident occurs. A lot depends on the care exercised by the men who drive the jeeps. Tigers that are irritated for some reason do charge the jeeps but they have always been mock charges and have never culminated in an attack. In fact once a tigress whom we named Nasty charged me over a dozen times in a period of a few months. Actually it comes as a shock. The jeeps are open on the sides and top and to be confronted by a snarling, growling tiger less than a metre away is paralysing. It is only after years of experience that one learns to accept this possibility and an observer has to be careful to select the best position for a jeep without being intrusive or threatening. Our greatest concern was that if a group of people teased or chased a family of tigers, then they may have to face the wrath of a tigress. We humans have a certain sense of arrogance in such situations. An arrogance born of fear. This is what is dangerous.

In the summer of 1988 the Semli cubs were into their adult life. Usually when we saw them they were alone; we only occasionally encountered them as a group. They seemed to sustain their links as siblings. Noon's cubs were nearly two years old. The male was spending most of his time alone, but continuing to join mother and sister over food. His sister spent more time with Noon. Unlike leopards, tiger cubs spend nearly twenty months in close touch with the mother. Leopard cubs tend to become independent between the ages of twelve and fourteen months. But with tigers the process of becoming independent occurs differently for different cubs and depends on the nature and individual characteristics of the cub. I think it is also affected by the ecological system in which they live. If undisturbed and well managed, tigers can, as families, form temporary groupings in order to hunt and share food. There is, of course, much myth surrounding the tiger's solitary nature. I think tigers were forced into solitary and nocturnal lives in order to survive their endless persecution. In protected and undisturbed habitats like Ranthambhore the tiger has flourished and revealed facets of its family life that few would have imagined possible. They live in family groups that maintain links even after the cubs reach adulthood, thus demonstrating the possibility of sustaining kin links over long periods of time. Throughout this period of two years we never observed, or saw any evidence of, conflict between the growing cubs and the resident male. There is no doubt that the resident male who fathers the litter plays a role in raising the family.

We had been fortunate to see the cubs of Noon, Laxmi and Nalghati, seven in all, reach a point of maturity where they could kill for themselves. The Basandhra cubs around the fringe had not been so lucky. One of the cubs had presumably been poisoned soon after feeding on a buffalo carcass. The Bakaula tigress who operated in the resident Bakaula male's range had been seen briefly with two cubs. But during a period of three months in early 1988 she suffered from a severe wound in her right paw that caused her much anguish and pain. Somehow she limped around and managed to kill the occasional chital and sambar for her cubs. But the state of the wound restricted effective hunting. She would lick it frequently, her saliva being an excellent antiseptic. I couldn't believe that she could cure it. It had been bloody one day, but improved and was soon back to normal. But during this period she had lost a twelve-month-old cub and was now seen with only one cub.

Ensuring the survival of the cubs is a difficult process. The mother loses a few cubs at birth and then when the offspring are six months old, with a burgeoning appetite, a lot depends on the availability of prey, the size of the litter and the mother's abilities. This can be a vulnerable time and a cub can sometimes be lost in the frenzied quest for food. When sub-adult tigers are independent and hunting they can suffer from a lack of skill and experience. This is a moment when their mother's training determines their chances of survival in the future. At this final stage the father's role is minimal. From the time when the cubs are sixteen to eighteen months old the father's presence is irregular and interactions with the sub-adult cubs rare.

Our final observation of family life was late one afternoon during the middle of May 1988 with Noon in the Rajbagh area. It was a memorable evening. At that time of year the water of the lake has receded to a shallow tract in the centre. Chital herds congregated on the open ground to feed on the green shoots at the water's edge. At 5.30 that

Noon's two year old cubs soon after feeding on the carcass of a sambar hind. The male cub's face is covered in blood. The cubs nuzzle each other, relaxed and satiated. Contact between the siblings and Noon continued into their third year. Unlike Laxmi's cubs, who were leading separate lives by this age, Noon's tended to interact with their mother more often. This may be because their territory was smaller and the concentration of prey forced them together over food.

Kublai, the resident male, and Noon's female cub, now two years old, at a water hole. Kublai slaps a wet paw on the cub's face. It is rare to see such interaction between adult tigers – it is a test of dominance with the male asserting his strength and power.

evening the male cub emerged from a bank of high grass. Well fed and fit, he walked leisurely towards the water. The chital herds alarm called, watching him carefully. But he was in no mood to hunt. The herd moved to give way to him. A few sambar in the water alarm called and walked out. The chital watched the tiger at the edge of the water as he settled in to cool himself and quench his thirst. They then went back to grazing without further alarm. The tiger sat quietly soaking in the water. Thirty minutes later Noon emerged from the far side and headed to the water, reclining in it opposite her cub. Soon afterwards the female cub appeared and strolled up to the water, immersing herself in it some thirty metres from Noon. All three tigers sat. The chital herd grazed in the background. The sun was setting. It was my last day. The saga of the families was over. I wondered what the monsoons would be like. Would the crocodiles survive? What would the lakes be like? Would all three tigers be active in the following season? Their level of predation around the lakes was high. Would the lakes be able to sustain enough prey after the rain? The key factor in determining their future would be the success of the rains. I prayed for it.

The End of A Century

At the turn of this century there were possibly 40,000 tigers in India. Vast tracts of the country were carpeted with a variety of forests in which the tiger flourished. The population of man was, then, hundreds of million less.

Today, nearly a hundred years later, we get ready to enter the 21st century. The official figure of tiger numbers is around 4,500. Since census operations suffer from large margins of error I do not believe this figure. I think it is more likely to be 3,000, and this in the rapidly diminishing forests which now cover only eight per cent of the country's land mass. The human population has passed 800 million. The population of domestic livestock is 1.7 billion. There is incredible pressure on the natural resources of this country from both man and livestock.

The tiger has little chance of survival against this onslaught. In fact I feel that for the first time since the initial success of Project Tiger, tiger populations have stabilised and in some cases started to decrease. In Ranthambhore, the tiger population has remained around forty for the last four years. Populations of tigers can only increase when the area of forests that they live in increase. When this does not happen, tigers control their own population by fatal disputes among themselves over food and territory.

Habitats for the tiger are shrinking or being degraded, some turning into islands like Ranthambhore. The alienation of rural communities from the wilderness areas around them is total. The government's task is nearly impossible. But then they are directly responsible for the problem. A lack of foresight has created a tiger crisis, as when our forests are endangered, the tiger is threatened too.

If we want to prevent our wilderness areas from becoming safari parks then there is a ten per cent chance that wild India will survive, if that. There are about 450 national parks, sanctuaries and wildlife areas in India protected by constitutional rules and regulations. I think that in India we have reached a level of saturation regarding what we can protect. There is little point in adding to this long list. We must protect and preserve for the future certain specific areas in India, a carefully chosen hundred of them, rather than wasting resources and administrative potential on all 450. Let us concentrate our energies, financial and otherwise, on protecting fewer areas more effectively. These areas must include viable units with connecting corridors to other areas, thereby ensuring healthy genetic pools, and in all such protection efforts the human habitations around the wilderness must be taken into account. They must be a part of the total protection and management effort, well

OVERLEAF:
An unusual Ranthambhore scene. Noon's male cub walks across the rapidly drying waters of Rajbagh to cool himself. Two sambar stags watch his progress cautiously, tails raised in alarm. A large herd of chital in the background carries on grazing; a few of them watch the tiger but none raises an alarm. They seem to know intuitively that the tiger is heading for water and is not interested in an attack.

149

integrated into a conservation strategy for the future.

Unfortunately, in India, such planning and implementation has not taken place at all. The Project Tiger management plans failed to take into consideration the plight and concerns of the people living around a reserve. In Ranthambhore, though the resettlement of the villages from inside the park to the outside was effective, it still failed to be an ongoing process of continuing vital links and relationships with the village populations. In the last decade the relationship between the park management and the rural communities has become severely strained and under pressure. The villagers should have been made more aware of the importance of the forest as a wild habitat, and efforts should have been made to reduce their need to encroach on it. As each month rolls by it becomes more difficult to cement such a relationship. If Ranthambhore, its tigers and tigresses and cubs and all the other wild inhabitants are to survive into the 21st century, immediate steps must be taken to implement schemes for rural populations. This is the only way genuine and serious conservation of this area is possible.

The following are the kind of schemes that would strengthen the links between the people and the wilderness areas they live around. This is, in my opinion, the only way to recreate the traditional harmony between man and nature and restore the threads of this intricate texture which is essential to the survival of both.

1. Ranthambhore is like an island surrounded by enormous populations of cattle and human beings. This exerts tremendous pressure on the park. One of the schemes to relieve this pressure involves dairy development, cattle care and artificial insemination programmes which will increase milk yields and generate income. It is essential to encourage the village to set up dairy co-operatives ensuring an equitable milk distribution. The cattle must be cared for and their potential developed.

2. It is essential in Ranthambhore to preserve the vegetal cover in the fringe areas of the forest. This will only be possible with a concerted effort by the villagers themselves. Village co-operatives must be set up and then helped to acquire and develop alternative pasture lands for grazing. The benefits of stall feeding must be stressed, and methods of increasing fodder production implemented. Replanting of trees through the setting up of effective nurseries and organised social forestry programmes is essential.

3. The encouragement of alternative technologies that act to relieve the pressure on a forest are vital. It is essential that

villages in the forest areas find alternative fuel instead of burning firewood. Smokeless cookers that cut firewood requirements by fifty per cent should be made available. Biogas plants must be set up to eliminate the need for firewood completely. Alternative energy systems such as solar thermal systems must be promoted.

4. Fundamental problems of rural poverty can only be resolved by income generation programmes. Traditional skills must be used to add to household earnings and handicrafts of the region must be promoted to supplement the income of the women staying at home. This income would lift a great burden from the forest, as when unoccupied, most women spend much of their time cutting grass for fodder in the forest, depleting a vital natural resource that can have severe repercussions for the inhabitants of the forest. The increase in income may help them to buy fodder at subsidised rates from fodder depots.

5. Mother and child health care is also vital if the living conditions of the people are to improve. This will encompass immunisation schemes, health, education and supplementary feeding of malnourished children, as well as promoting family planning, which is vital for the future. Basic medicines and first aid facilities must be made easily available.

6. With all this activity it is critical that there be educational programmes to increase awareness of the problem. Such programmes with posters, information sheets, films and audio-visuals will aid in the conservation of the area.

Important forest areas like Ranthambhore cannot survive without the collective co-operation of the people who live there. Measures like the above will assist in vital areas like ground water preservation, to which governments have paid scant attention, choosing instead to develop expensive and sometimes harmful large irrigation projects. Ground water is independent and a natural gift that accounts for 98 per cent of all fresh water reserves throughout the world. Unless supplies are replenished, water tables will fall due to overpumping and deforestation. We need a stronger forestry research base and the direct involvement of the people to resolve a most difficult problem, that of the unrestricted grazing of livestock. It is the unbearable pressure that these animals exert on the land which is responsible for the wholesale destruction of young trees and grass before they get a chance to establish themselves: left strictly alone, thanks to the seeds carried in the air, bird droppings, bees and butterflies, natural vegetation re-asserts itself rapidly, even in the most inhospitable conditions. The closing of denuded land to grazing offers the quickest and most inex-pensive way to restore vegetal cover.

For this, re-education and mobilising the people is essential but vil-lagers will only give freely of their time and labour if they perceive the work to be for their common good and know that the benefits will therefore be shared in a fair and equitable way. It is here that non-governmental organisations have a vital role to play in helping the people to manage their basic natural resources. This is what will ultimately determine whether future generations of tigers can survive in our wilds.

India has an amazing diversity of habitat and there is a corresponding variety and richness in the flora and fauna. It also has an enormous human population. Both somehow have managed against tremendous odds. But for how long? Each area in India faces its own set of problems. For long term conservation to be successful specific situations need to be examined and a series of different action plans implemented through the length and breadth of the country so that man and nature can live together in harmony.

Taking all the above into consideration, a group of concerned people have recently created the Ranthambhore Foundation in an attempt to focus directly on the area around the park and help to resolve some of its most severe problems so that this precious piece of forest will survive into yet another century. And not only this area but also the wilderness of India as a whole. It is only by preserving a viable population of tigers all over our subcontinent that nature and all its inhabitants can survive.

India is now recognised as a force in terms of technological and scientific development and application. At the same time, we should be critical of what we have failed to grasp and implement with regard to social development. The government has ignored our people, their surroundings, their suffering, the lack of even the most basic needs of life which affects the majority of our population.

Problems associated with personal and environmental hygiene, com-pounded by a lack of education and the inability of our service infrastructure to provide such basic human needs as regular safe drink-ing water, sanitation and energy, perpetuate poor health and a degrad-ing form of living for too many people.

Burgeoning population growth is undermining and negating much of our economic and industrial progress. The pressures created by over-crowding and competition for space have placed an immense burden on the land, natural resources and our unique natural and cultural heritage.

India is not alone in having to face these problems. The world's whole ecosystem is threatened by the exploitation of irreplaceable natural areas and resources. Pollution of every kind is on the increase. Every day the planet loses species that are gone forever, adding to an inevitable breakdown in our delicate natural balance.

Within these realities there exist tremendous possibilities for change and achievement. Immediate human survival concerns will always take precedence over long term environmental goals, but there must be an awareness that the broader struggle to achieve a social order in which the needs of all are met, must go hand in hand with an ecological balance.

Man is today creating the seeds of his own downfall and destruction. Numerous forms of life are slowly disappearing from this planet of which they are an integral part. Man and every living organism that makes up this world are interlocked in a complex and delicate matrix of life like the threads of a tapestry. If one strand breaks, the matrix is weakened and man draws closer to the disintegration of his habitat and therefore himself. So let us act quickly before it is too late.

Noon's cubs on an old fort wall late in the evening. This particular wall was one of the main entrance gates to the fort and in times gone by must have been one of its major defences. Noon's home range is dotted with old walls, ruined temples and mosques, chatris, tombs, and even a summer palace. The cubs spend a lot of time around these ruins, exploring them and using them as day shelters.

Postscript

In 1988 the Ranthambhore National Park experienced one of the best rainfalls in 25 years. A severe drought is over. All the reservoirs are brimming full of water. The monsoon has regenerated the entire forest and saved it from what might have been a major crisis. But all the news is not good.

One of the saddest events in Ranthambhore's history occurred in September 1988. One of the cubs of the Basandhra tigress, active on the fringes of the forest, killed a seven-year-old boy and ate part of the body. It is the first case of man-eating recorded in Ranthambhore. The tiger is being carefully tracked to see whether this was an isolated incident or whether it threatens to kill again. If it does, it will be tranquillised and removed to a zoo or put to sleep.

What is not in doubt is that this young tiger, aged 28 months, had endured intensive disturbance from livestock, tourists and pilgrims. The incident happened on the day of the annual Ganesh fair, when over 20,000 pilgrims walk up towards the fort. The tiger, waiting to cross the road to get to a water hole at 7.30 in the evening, was impeded by this great procession and in desperation, attacked the boy he found in his way. This deviation from his natural behaviour was a direct result of finding his home and his normal activities threatened. It is a tragic example of the way human disturbance can disturb the precious balance between man and nature.

January 1989. A cold winter's morning. The drive into the forest was numbing. The first light of day was creeping over the horizon as I turned towards the main entrance of the park. Suddenly, on a looming cliff, I saw the silhouette of a cat's head. A leopard sat on the edge grooming itself at dawn. We moved on a few hundred metres into the park to find the Basandhra tigress sitting at the edge of the road. My heart missed a beat as she was suddenly joined by first one, then another and finally a third cub about eight months old. The cubs jumped and cuddled her nervously and she soon led them across the road towards thicker forest.

A few days earlier she had been seen with not only these three cubs but also the female cub of her earlier litter. They were all moving around together as a family. This was amazing.

The Basandhra tigress gave birth to a litter in early May 1986. By December 1987 the cubs, one male and one female, had left their mother. The male cub was found, probably poisoned, near the carcass of a buffalo in December 1987. These are the sad consequences for tigers that are active near the fringe areas of a forest.

The forest in the monsoon. Water cascades down the cliffs and the forest swells with water, turning a vibrant green. Water rushes down hillsides to fill water holes, lakes and dry stream beds. The forest is suddenly crisscrossed by gurgling streams and gushing, muddy rivers. The fury of water and its magical regeneration of the forest are remarkable.

157

The Basandhra tigress conceived again during February 1988, maybe a couple of months after her cubs had left her. She delivered a new litter in May 1988. It was probably the female cub of her earlier litter who accidentally killed the young boy. But what was remarkable was the fact that the cubs of both litters were meeting at times, and sustaining their links.

That same morning I noticed crows and vultures very near the original den that Noon had moved her young cubs to. Sightings of Noon and her cubs, now 31 months, had been erratic over the last few months. The cubs were found, sometimes alone, and sometimes with Noon, especially over a kill. But in the last few months they had been seen only once in ten days around the lakes. They all seemed to come back nearly every day to the vicinity of the den.

Later that afternoon Fateh saw vultures circling and decided to investigate. The forest provided another of its surprises. Beneath the vultures were the remnants of the bones of a chital. Noon sat twenty metres away and Fateh had a flashing glimpse of two, two month old cubs as they fled into a bush. The picture cleared. Noon's absences were explained. She had conceived her second litter when her cubs were 25 or 26 months old and delivered her litter in November 1988 when her cubs were 29 months old.

Pugmark evidence of the last few months indicated the regular presence of tigers near Jogi Mahal. There was no doubt that again

Early one morning in February 1989. Noon carries her six week old cub in her mouth. The second cub (out of picture) scampers behind. A tigress carries her cubs this way to ensure their safety when moving them to a more secure den. This behaviour has very rarely been photographed in the wild. We thank A. V. N. Jaggarow for permitting us to use this picture – he was the only person who observed this activity in Ranthambhore.

Noon, her 31 month old cubs and her two month old cubs were all spending time together. A rare and new facet of the secret life of tigers had been revealed. It was new information on the natural oestrus cycles and reproductive behaviour. Most importantly, we had two examples of how cubs of past and present litters do come together and sustain their kin links over a period of time.

We have no information on who fathered the Basandhra tigress's litter. Nor do we have information on who fathered Noon's litter. Since the monsoon in October 1988 Kublai has disappeared from the area of the lakes. If there is a new resident male he has not been seen with any regularity.

At the time of writing, one of Laxmi's female cubs, now about three years old, is seen often in her home range between Lakarda and Kachida. She was last sighted as she protected two kills, a young chital fawn and a langur monkey! There are occasional sightings of Laxmi's male cub in his mother's range but few sightings of the second female cub. The Nalghati male cub is seen often in Nalghati. The female's presence is irregular. The good news is that the Basandhra tigress's female cub has not attacked anyone else and the September incident seems to have been an isolated one.

Laxmi's female cub mates with a young male. She is now an adult, 38 months old and the resident tigress of the Lakarda valley. This is the first record of her mating. We thank Tejbir Singh for permission to use this picture.

Further Reading

Baikov, N.A. *The Manchurian Tiger* (Hutchinson, London, 1925)

Baker, S. *Wild Beasts and their Ways* (London, 1890)

Baze, W. *Tiger, Tiger* (London, 1957)

Biscoe, W. *A tiger killing a panther*, Journal of the Bombay Natural History Society 9(4): 490 (1895)

Brander, A.A. Dunbar. *Wild Animals in Central India (Edward Arnold, London, 1923)*

Campbell, T. *A tiger eating a bear*, Journal of the Bombay Natural History Society 9(1): 101 (1894)

Champion, F.W. *With Camera in Tiger Land* (Chatto & Windus, London, 1927)

Champion, F.W. *The Jungle in Sunlight and Shadow* (Chatto & Windus, London, 1933)

Corbett, G. *A tiger attacking elephants*, Journal of the Bombay Natural History Society (7)1: 192 (1892)

Corbett, J. *Man Eaters of Kumaon* (Oxford University Press, Oxford, 1944)

Courtney, N. *The Tiger, Symbol of Freedom* (Quartet, London, 1980)

Gee, E.P. *The Wildlife of India* (Collins, London, 1964)

Ghorpade, M.Y. *Sunlight and Shadows* (Gollancz, London, 1983)

Hanley, P. *Tiger Trails in Assam* (Robert Hale, London, 1961)

Krishnan, M. *India's Wildlife in 1959–70* (Bombay, 1975)

Littledale, H. *Bears being eaten by tigers*, Journal of the Bombay Natural History Society 4(4): 316 (1889)

Locke, A. *The Tigers of Trengganu* (London, 1954)

Mcdougal, C. *The Face of the Tiger* (Rivington Books, London, 1977)

Morris, R. *A tigress with five cubs*, Journal of the Bombay Natural History Society 31(3): 810–11 (1927)

Mountfort, G. *Tigers* (David and Charles, London, 1973)

Mountfort, G. *Back from the Brink* (Hutchinson, London, 1978)

Mountfort, G. *Saving the Tiger* (Michael Joseph, London, 1981)

Musselwhite, A. *Behind the Lens in Tiger Land* (London, 1933)

Perry, R. *The World of the Tiger* (Cassell & Co. Ltd., London, 1964)

Rathore, Singh and Thapar. *With Tigers in the Wild* (Vikas Publishing, Delhi, 1983)

Richardson, W. *Tiger Cubs*, Journal of the Bombay Natural History Society 5(2): 191 (1890)

Saharia, V.B. *Wildlife in India* (Delhi, 1982)

Sanderson, G.P. *Thirteen Years Among the Wild Beasts of India* (W.H. Allen & Co., London, 1982)

Sankhala, K. *Tiger* (Collins, London, 1978)

Schaller, G. *The Deer and the Tiger* (University of Chicago Press, 1967)

Scott, Jonathan. *The Leopard's Tale* (Elm Tree Books, London, 1985)

Seshadri, B. *The Twilight of India's Wild Life* (John Baker, London, 1969)

Shahi, S.P. *Backs to the Wall* (Delhi, 1977)

Singh, A. *Tiger Haven* (Macmillan, London, 1973)

Singh, A. *Tara, a Tigress* (Quartet, London, 1981)

Singh, A. *Tiger Tiger* (Jonathan Cape, London 1984)

Singh, K. *The Tiger of Rajasthan* (London, 1959)

Singh, K. *Hints on Tiger Shooting* (The Hindustan Times Ltd., Delhi, 1965)

Stebbing, E.P. *Jungle By-ways in India* (London, 1911)

Stracey, P.D. *Tigers* (Barker, London, 1968)

Sunquist, Fiona and Mel. *Tiger Moon* (University of Chicago Press, 1988)

Thapar, Valmik. *Tiger: Portrait of a Predator* (Collins, London, 1986)

Toogood, C. *Number of cubs in a tigress' litter*, Journal of the Bombay Natural History Society 39(1): 158 (1936)

Toovey, J. *Tigers of the Raj* (Alan Sutton, London, 1987)

For further information about Ranthambhore National Park, write to The Ranthambhore Foundation, 19 Kautilya Marg, Chanakyapuri, New Delhi 110 021; or The Ranthambhore Society (a registered British charity), Grantchester, Linden Gardens, Leatherhead, Surrey, KT22 7HB.

All photographs by Fateh Singh Rathore except: pages 11, 16, 20, 24 (both photos), 60, 61 (bottom), 63, 64, 83 (both photos), 84–85, 86 (both photos), 87 (both photos), 88–89, 90 (both photos), 92, 93 120, 156 by Valmik Thapar; pages 50, 68, 116, 159 by Tejbir Singh; and p. 158 by A.V.N. Jaggarow.